SUPERNATURALZ:

WEIRD CREEPY &

RANDOM

(A NOVEL)

Ben Parris

William Freedman

Polus Books

PB

New York

SUPERNATURALZ: WEIRD CREEPY & RANDOM

(A NOVEL)

This edition was produced by Polus Books

Published in the United States of America

ISBN: 1942183003

ISBN-13: 978-1-942183-00-6

Forward

From the Director of the movie, Supernaturalz: Weird, Creepy & Random:

Horror is a natural for comedy. *Young Frankenstein* is one of my favorites, as is *The Rocky Horror Picture Show*. No wonder I was inspired to direct my own horror-comedy, *Supernaturalz: Weird, Creepy & Random*, a homage to 1950's juvenile delinquent movies like the campy *Teenage Hellcats* and 1970's grindhouse movies such as the edgy *Switchblade Sisters*.

I previously directed the documentaries, *Vampira: The Movie*, and *The Wild World of Ted V. Mikels*, with my filmmaking school behind the walls of Troma Entertainment. In other words, Troma's Lloyd Kaufman was my Yoda. And like Yoda, he was on my back until I learned something.

The plot of *Supernaturalz: Weird, Creepy & Random* is set in Salem, Massachusetts, which is still a misunderstood place, as are those they called witches. When the first Salem witch trials in the 1600's fueled the fascination with the supernatural, it said more about the town than its more exotic residents. The rituals of witches and ancient spells reach into the earliest of civilizations. The truth of it is, historians are finding that much of the mysticism goes back to ancient Indian culture, so adding the element of Hinduism to the story is a fitting touch.

I believe in the supernatural. I do. The existence of

the novel itself is as "spooky" as Albert Einstein's estimation of the world of Quantum Physics. #nocoincidence

I am a big fan of William Castle, who made many movies that shocked audiences like *The Tingler* and *The House on Haunted Hill*, and *13 Ghosts*, and I had hoped that we could have put similar "gimmicks" into the viewing of the movie, *Supernaturalz: Weird, Creepy & Random*. We wanted to have the characters in the movie text audience members and let the audience text back. The technology to provide that sort of flourish is not here yet. (So now I'm leaving it up to Brett Ratner or James Gunn.)

Now we have this novel that you hold in your hands (in solid form or ebook), and you can text while reading it. I would suggest, however, that you read it with the lights on.

The novel provides more details about the Garter Snakes Gang, their car theft, their criminal motivations, and the history of Kali. These girls are violent creatures, and as it goes in most plots, they get punished for their wrongful deeds. We can only sit back and enjoy the carnage.

At the end of this book you will find the continuation of the story. If you can't wait for the next installment, and you have a ghost of a chance, read it twice. It could be its own sequel.

Kevin Sean Michaels

October, 2014

Prologue
Kali and Hanu

Sanjivani's name meant immortality, and names had power, so why was she dying? Because there was a name more powerful than hers by far. She made her son, Sardar, lean in close to get her last words. More like one word.

For Sardar, it was if the blade of Kali, the sword of enlightenment, whisked past his ear when she whispered Kali's name, and he thought he could see the letters in Sanskrit six feet high in front of him, saying, "Kala," which is Time itself. Time and Death, on which the goddess was founded, were nebulous concepts for Sardar, but Evil was too real. He would have thought that only a serpent's tongue could say the name of Kali. Yet Sardar's mother said it softly as she lay dying. Time had run out, and death had come to claim her. Primordial Kali, severing the ego, releasing the soul. Kali, the Dark Mother, was eternal.

The Horror. Sardar's imagination went into overdrive. The human ego resides in the head, so Kali took heads and wore them on her belt. It was the visions again, Sardar's rare, extravagant, mind shattering glimpses... but the dark force of Kali was no myth.

Centuries before Christ, around 500 BCE, Sardar's ancestor, a devotee of Lord Shiva himself, battled with the Dark Mother. This ancestor's name was Hanu, a yogi.

The Dark Mother was evil. The ancient Hindus suffered the carnage as Mother Kali took monstrous form, killing everything in its path like a malevolent tornado. Yet

Kali was loved and She served a higher purpose to protect her children—the good ones.

Hanu saw her, midnight blue Mother Kali, who appeared adorned with a garland of fifty human heads and a skirt of animal skin and dismembered arms. While Kali hacked the evil-doers with her sword, so also did She slay the innocents. Hanu could not reconcile her duality. She was like a fireball that made no distinctions.

He reported what he had witnessed to Lord Shiva at the Temple in the Mountains. But Lord Shiva took no action, instead explaining the wisdom of Kali to Hanu, who tried to listen patiently.

"She destroys ignorance and inertia," Lord Shiva explained. "In essence, she is killing this reality in order to forge a new future for the Hindus."

"Why do so many good people have to die in order to achieve this new future?" the puzzled Hanu asked his master.

"Evil has its place," the master replied. "It's inseparable from good."

Days passed and entire villages burned to the ground. Bodies piled up everywhere and the blood pooled into a river. Hanu decided he had seen enough bloodshed and entered the fray against the bloodthirsty mistress. Kali's name crowded out everything else in his mind. He ignored Lord Shiva's words, replacing wisdom with his anger.

Kali appeared at the entrance of The Temple in the Mountains as though summoned by Hanu. He challenged Kali with his limited knowledge of spells and magic, expending flares of pyrotechnics against her, which were impressive only to mortal witnesses. Kali pushed Hanu aside as though he were puny and entered the Temple whereupon Hanu closed and sealed the heavy door behind Her. What he forgot was that Lord Shiva was inside too.

Lord Shiva was forced to confront Kali, who was content to destroy the sacred scrolls inside, which would plunge the Hindus into a dark age. She stomped the scrolls to dust, but before She could crush them all, Lord Shiva threw his body under Her feet. Kali stuck Her tongue out and hissed like a dragon. Lord Shiva called upon the power of Brahmin, and the two of them froze in their place, one down, one up. The Temple door was sealed forever.

While the bloodshed was over, Hanu was sure that a curse had fallen over mankind from that day forward... because Kali's essence and her power would find another way out.

BEN PARRIS and WILLIAM FREEDMAN

Chapter 1
God of Everything

<u>Salem, Massachusetts, twenty-five years ago or more,</u>
<u>sometime in the '80's</u>

Passersby could hear the action from outside Bonnie's Bed and Breakfast. Even over the synth-pop blaring out of the stereo, a ruckus as crude as a rutting bull ape cut through the walls, across the vast lawn, and onto the other side of the garden gate.

Amidst a chorus of creaking, huffing and puffing in the darkness—reflecting the ecstasy of sloppy lovemaking—a man proclaimed, "I am the Mighty Sardar! I am the Mighty Sardar! I *am* the Mighty Sardar!" Then he broke loose with a half-assed Tarzan yell that degenerated into a coughing fit. Within a second, he was back to being just plain old Gary, a 26-year-old Indian guy living in the garage.

The girl underneath Gary in the dark was young, carefree Kris. She managed to squeak out, "Whatever." It was a popular word in that decade.

A major event had passed. Gary turned on a lamp on a side table. Out of breath in frigid drafts of New England morning air that swirled through the decrepit house's cellar, Gary lifted a joint that he had secreted in his turban along with a lighter. He'd had the turban on the whole time. Kris didn't mind. He thrusted like a king when it sat atop his head. Hoping to spark up, he flicked the wheel on the lighter twice without success. The flint didn't ignite. He was oblivious to the smoldering logs in the fireplace behind him and that was fortunate because he would probably have burned his face off trying to stick his head in it. Still, it's "420" time.

The couple had been using the mantle as a headboard for their bright-yellow sleeping bag, so cheery in an otherwise dank and drab hearth room. Even so, it fit in by smelling suitably musty, of mold and mothballs.

Over his shoulder, Kris peeked out, nearly nude except for warm socks.

"I want to be free! Live forever in this sleeping bag," came the twittering exclamation from pouty lips in a round face of rosy cheeks framed by dirty-blond hair under a leopard-skin headband.

"Calm down," said Gary. "I can't believe you have to do it with that ratty old sleeping bag wrapped around you like a mummy. It's gross."

"It's my mom's. She doesn't miss it when I borrow it."

"Double gross!" Gary's charcoal eyes glared out over the circular rims of retro-styled tinted specs. "I don't want her finding out about us. Then I'll get kicked out of here."

"When are you leaving anyway?"

Focused back on the task of getting the doobie lit, he said, "I am only staying in this house as long as your Dad allows me."

Kris gave him the sly look of a raccoon. "Did that deal come with sleeping with his fifteen-year-old daughter?"

A hard swallow from The Mighty Sardar.

Kris sat up and popped half out of the bag. Her breasts, exposed to the chill, prickled with gooseflesh as she reached for her green shirt and tugged it on. A red, serpentine bauble hung from her leather necklace, nuzzling in her cleavage.

Gary looked at her all too familiar form, then promptly looked away and shrugged. He knew she was young, but somewhere in the back of his mind he wanted her to be magically eighteen. Yet the accusation was all too true.

"I'd better not develop those pictures I took," he joked as he buttoned up his denim work shirt. "Besides, if I deflowered you, your Dad with his crazy temper had better not know it." Her dad, Burl, had a nasty side and anything was possible if he discovered there was a rooster in the hen house.

Then Gary's thoughts shifted to her more liberal mother. "Your mom definitely wouldn't mind. She looks like she's had a lot of life experience," Gary said. "Not to be mean, but she looks old enough to have a kid in college. She's aging in dog years lately."

"No kidding! I don't know what's up with her. She's gotten so obsessed and desperate about her age, she'll do absolutely anything to get young again."

"Forever young, huh? That's not possible," Gary chuckled.

No, it is not possible. But that does not keep people from trying. While most use exercise or diet or even surgery to stem decrepitude, others rely on darker arts. The results may be surer, but they require constant attention. If demonic forces are not constantly assuaged, they have their ways of demanding their due. Go off the diet and, over the course of weeks, you get thicker in the middle. Break training, and in a few months you'll have flab hanging off your bones. If surgery is unsuccessful, you get stretch marks where your wrinkles would be. But fail to appease a demon, and the results are dramatic and immediate.

Out on the grounds but hidden by the woods, a small fire burned in the twilight. Above it sat an altar, supporting a lidded, rosewood box.

Kris's mom, Dawn, was indeed willing to try anything short of selling her own soul. She was too caught up in her belief in black magic, regardless of all consequence.

A flurry of smoke billowed and Dawn fed it a powder. The mixture responded with a shimmering pulse. But dramatic potions would not be enough. She could see her flaking skin fluttering off her face in the heat. She picked at scabs as large as her fingers. If she had spent a week in the Sahara without shade, maybe her cheeks might have peeled like this. But they would be red, enflamed. Instead, the pile of dead tissue collecting around the fire pit was frigid and pale. With each such session, she reverted to a worsened state, making her desperate to do more and more of what the spirits demanded of her, stripping away her humanity in the process.

She hated looking so diminished. The drive to restore youthful vibrancy to that face, the one that generations ago inspired the lust of a young man of property and brought her a life of comfort— to protect the continued attentions of Burl, a superficial man with a wandering eye. The face that her young Kris was fortunate to be growing into. The face that she often caught the handsome seasonal helper Gary gazing into admiringly. This is more than vanity. Her whole world lay in the balance.

Dawn wore a stylish dress of the 1980's, a non-representational print in blue. Her hair was dark and — in a year where frizzy hair was actually in vogue – alluring. But the parts of her face left intact were sagging in lines and folds.

Waving a staff high in a circular motion over the carved wooden box, she incanted a hymn to an ancient evil. "Kreem…kreem…kreem…hoom hoom…"

Dawn lowered her voice to a whisper. Kali would hear her prayers, for she was the goddess that Dawn invoked with her cloying mantra. Kali of Time. Kali of Death.

Gyrations accompanied the chant, along with circular motions with the huge, crimson, ovoid stone that a thick-banded ring tethered to her finger. In the generations of vanity that have kept this tradition from moldering into superstition, only the hairstyle and wardrobe changed. Witches in fashion.

How is it that no one in the town put two-and-two together that Dawn Marten, was in fact the very same person who built the Marten House in 1923 in a secluded section of Salem, Massachusetts? How is it that it went unnoticed that a series of "cousins," "daughters" and possibly granddaughters supposedly lived in the house over the more than half a century it stood, and shockingly resembled the same woman— a thirty-year-old siren, all passing down the name of Dawn?

When Dawn met Burl Bonnie in 1973, she told him that she had just inherited the enormous mansion with almost no cash to run it. Her grandfather's will said she couldn't sell it, putting her in an untenable bind. Dropping the hint that it would take an impossible amount of money to transform a care-worn, charming mansion into a slick hotel, she let Burl think it was his idea to turn it into a bed and breakfast and put his name on it. B&Bs were the hot new trend but the average ones could only service a few people at a time. While Burl knew he could never fill Dawn's place, he had the capacity for as many people as tourist season could bring. Most importantly, with the young temptress thrown into the deal as his wife, he got Marten House for free. Might as well use it all.

Back at the house, Kris stirred in the sleeping bag until she let out a painful "Ow!"

Gary's sense of priorities kept him from acknowledging Kris's outburst.

"Mom left one of her damn statues in the bottom of the bag," Kris explained. "I just got a...a paper cut." She tossed it out and it settled upright on the marbled base of the fireplace.

Gary turned for a moment to identify the offending metal figure. The color of unadorned brown-dirt clay, the statue — a foot-tall statuette, really— was the graven image of a many-armed deity in a conical helmet.

His shirt buttoned sloppily, his gaze fixated on a comic book that a boy half his age would not find challenging, he tried to be nonchalant but came across aggrieved at the interruption. "That's Shiva."

Kris, still thoroughly annoyed, said, "Which is what?"

"God of … Everything. What was your mom going to do…?"

Kris settled back down and shrugged her bare shoulders against its faux-satin lining.

"Does she plan to sacrifice a virgin to stay young?" he continued with a chortle. "You're safe from that now."

The fire still burning elsewhere, Dawn continued conjuring over the box atop the fire. Her gestures flowed with ever-greater animation as the rhythm quickened. At the end of her staff was the image of a wide, sleepy eye. Its blue, unblinking gaze locked on Dawn as she attempted to supplicate the demonic spirit it represented. "Kreem…kreem…kreem…hoom hoom…"

Something is wrong, she pondered. *The transformation should have occurred by now. I should no longer be here. I should be* …

As Gary got engrossed in his post-coital comic book, *Elvira's Tales of Mystery,* Kris was yanked down into the bag by an unnatural force.

Gary heard her rustling and figured that she was still horny. Sometimes girls liked to go for Round Two. By themselves. He was a typical man, glad that his work was over.

Terror seized her physically as well as emotionally, overwhelmed by the sensation of a tendril wrapping around her abdomen and midriff. Unable to speak, unable to scream, a mild "Ohhh!" rushed involuntarily from her lips.

With his eyes glued to the adventures in those illustrated pages, Gary responded pensively, "You make noises, girl. Yes, you do."

She thrashed fearfully in the bag that suddenly had no exit. She knew there was air in there. Yes, the bag stank, but the smell of mildew, semen and, yes, her own virginal blood were better than no air at all. Struggling against the forces that clamped her, Kris cleared her mind and found her voice. "Gary! Hey!"

"I love it when you say my name! Damn, this is good weed. I didn't even light it up and I'm having flashbacks from five minutes ago."

Five minutes ago she was rapt in one of the great pleasures of her life and now she feared she could count that one as her last. With each catching breath she bit off her complaints in halting screeches. One last time she vocalized, "Gary!" And then all she could manage was a weak "Urk!"

"An aftershock. What can I say? I'm a stud muffin," he bragged, arms raised in triumph, taking credit for what was hopefully an unexpected orgasm.

Sadly for Kris, this was no orgasm. One last scream followed by a final gasp and his tortured companion fell limp.

He finally turned around to regard her with disdain and then resignation. "So she gets the goods and then just conks out? Her daddy's going to kill me. I'd better get out of here."

Hurriedly, with only the statuette to keep sentry

watch over the room, Gary left her passed out in the sleeping bag on the cold floor, the serpentine charm pointing like a dagger at her throat. It never occurred to him to check if she was still breathing. All he remembered was to grab the large jar of M&M's.

I should be... home.

Magic has its limits, especially if you want to keep it a secret. As long as Gary remained in the presence of her daughter, Dawn could not intrude on that location. Still, as soon as Gary did clear the room, her hideous form claimed the space he vacated. Finding Kris a wet noodle in the bag, she tucked in an arm and some blonde hair, and with solemn ceremony delivered with a true believer's zeal, stuffed the eye club in the bag with Kris and closed it up.

Again, Dawn sensed that something was amiss with the spell. After her ministrations, the sacrifice should have been complete. She and her daughter – her offering – should be back in the woods, she figured, back at the makeshift altar over the simmering fire. Yet that was not the case. Had Kali rejected her gift? *No*, she told herself, *why would she do that to me?*

Instead, she deluded herself into thinking that the goddess merely demanded that she do the rest of the mule work herself. So Dawn dragged and bumped the makeshift body bag across the rolling hills of her property. She felt as if every step added another year of bone loss and disc decay to her searing spine. The backbreaking task took mere minutes that felt like hours. She could swear she saw her shadow shortening at the approach of midday.

Finally, she arrived back at the altar for a quick stop

to sprinkle the bag with powder. From there it was a short distance to the swampy pond. Its water – and here the definition of "water" was stretched – was green. A standing pool can be choked green with algae, but this swirling, gurgling puddle of slime reflected a hue that had little to do with the surrounding flora's shades of life.

After a quick and furtive look around, she heaved her daughter into the drink with a soupy splash. Mesmerized and perversely fascinated by what she had done, she stood and watched big bubbles form on the surface, smelled the swamp gases as they popped, and finally found herself a forked stick to prod with and made sure the bag sank deep.

"Kali, she's yours!"

That afternoon, when Gary went to check on Kris, he couldn't find her anywhere in the house and figured she must be outside. In the course of searching the ample grounds, he came to an area so woodsy that the bright daylight was swallowed in shadow. Not so much gloom though that he couldn't spy Burl through the trees, veins popping out of a forehead extended by encroaching baldness. Burl towered over someone obscured by the deep grass and shook with uncontrolled rage. His arms flailed, raining blows down on her. A woman's scream rose. Is that Kris? I hope not.

Gary wanted no part of it and he was too close already, but he stood rooted as the sound echoed and his vision blurred in and out. Occasionally, the female feet and hands flashed up defensively against her attacker's punches until Burl raised the Shiva statue, the very one Gary abandoned in his haste, to strike her.

"Don't!" she cried, the mother's voice and the daughter's voice so much alike, especially in a state a stress. It still could have been either of them. "No one has to know!"

But with a solid strike, Burl brought the statue down on the woman in the grass.

As he raised the bloodied object again, its jeweled crown glowed against a dimming background, the last thing Gary saw before passing out.

Chapter 2
It's Dangerous Not to Know

Salem, Massachusetts, a Nightclub, 25 Years Hence

An eerily similar jewel to the one in the statue of quarter-century ago shakes in the navel of a belly dancer. Its bearer is just one of a trio in the opening act of an ill-attended matinee for an Indian strip club, Sardar's, at the end of a mall in the far-flung, hardscrabble Boston suburb.

Sensuous, rhythmic *thumri* music plays as a few bored, boozy regulars nurse their bottom-shelf highballs. They barely notice, let alone provide an ovation, as the navel's owner and her two sisters finish their act. The ladies are not particularly good; in fact, they are purposely inferior to the main event to come.

On the tail of leering catcalls not meant for him, Sardar, a flashy, turbaned man in his fifties, strides out to do his mentalist act. The patrons moan, not too happy at the transition.

Confident that his showmanship can win out, the host enthuses, "Good evening. I am Sardar. The time has come to show you the most amazing acts ever seen on the stage."

An elderly barfly calls out, "Like what?"

Sardar locates the man. It's an old patron, someone Sardar can never please. "Do you want to see a girl cut in half?"

"No."

"A lady who must make a brave escape without air?"

"No."

"The collapsing box?"

"How about a snapping box," the man in the audience insists, his hands flapping to indicate a tightening vagina.

Thinking he's figured out a better hook this time, Sardar says, "How about this? The incredible Impaled Lady!"

The rest of the patrons join the lone heckler in booing and laughing at Sardar.

He lays down the law. "Hey, I am the owner of this place, so you cannot boo. I am the one who pays the bills and keeps the electric on. That should count for something. I mean I try so hard to keep everyone entertained and—"

"This is your act? Jesus Christ!"

"No, this is not my act. And I'm not Jesus Christ. As you well know, I am a magician and master of ceremonies."

"Then magically let my bar tab disappear."

The drummer does a rim shot, *ba-da-boom*, and hits the cymbal, topping it off with a sizzling chime.

Sardar grimaces with frustration that his own employee is playing along with his humiliation. He orders, "No drums for him. He's cut off. I mean, the heckler is in the audience. Only I get a drum roll."

"Bring on the titties," says the heckler.

"Soon," Sardar promises. "Now I will show you things beyond your comprehension."

"E.S.P.! E.S.P.!"

Sardar tries to oblige. "ESP now? Okay, think of a

21

number."

"No! I said, E.S.P.! Eat Shit, Prick!"

The drummer provides another rim shot.

"I can't believe I fell for that. The hell with it." Sardar claps once and the exotic dancer comes out swaying sensually. The patrons cheer.

Before he leaves the mike, Sardar raises one arm and says, "Introducing… Sultana!"

Promptly, Sultana gives them what the crowd requested— bouncing titties.

Backstage, a defeated Sardar brushes past his assistant, the twenty-something Marsha, with a listless wave for greeting. She has once again been playing around with the dancer's gear, this time a gold frilly vest.

Take off that stupid costume," he orders. Sardar is not in the mood for fun. He sits to take off his turban— just a prop for his act—and sighs.

Marsha saunters over to Sardar's desk, oblivious to his demeanor. "Sardar, do you think I'm ready to start my apprenticeship?"

Sardar looks at the mousy dark-blonde with a skeptic's appraisal. "Assistant manager maybe. Apprentice is a big step."

"But I want to learn everything, especially the mystic side. Not the phony tricks. The real stuff."

Sardar avoids eye contact, too busy doing little bits of business around his office. "You don't want to know that. It's dangerous."

"Maybe it's dangerous not to know. Did you ever think of *that?*"

Sardar gives her an impatient, dismissive wave. "In

time, Marsha. Certainly not now." They'd had this brisk, ritualized chat many times before.

Shaking with an outraged hiss, Marsha stalks past Sardar's book-lined shelves.

A woman closer to Sardar's age on her way into the dressing room thinks she will squeeze past Marsha in the confined space. Seeing the rage in Marsha's eyes, the woman flattens herself against the doorway as she enters.

To Sardar's back, the newcomer says, "Rough night, huh?"

Without looking, he responds, "Every night is a rough night here. It's a rough life."

"Not as rough as mine," she chides gently. "My daughter is missing."

Sardar, who is bored already, and busy on his computer, still does not stir to look at her. "Missing girl? You're in the wrong place. The dancers are in the other dressing room. Troubled girls shaking their titties, titties, titties. All of that bunch are the same to me. Why don't you pick out another girl at random and go on your way?"

The mystery woman covers his eyes. "No, Gary, it's me, Dawn."

Surprised, Gary realizes it's a long time since anyone called him by the name that was on his driver's license. Maybe on another night he might be more in the mood but, in that moment, he is not crazy about a surprise guest showing up. "Who calls me Gary? What Dawn?"

She uncovers his eyes.

"Oh, Dawn, what the hell! A ghost from the past. What are you doing here?"

"I'm out of jail."

Displeased to be reminded of those dark days, he says, "I see that. I'm sure you didn't come here for my act. It's not Gary anymore. It's The Mighty Sardar." Sardar sits in his swiveling makeup chair, off-loading his necklaces and rings to their various stations. He doesn't think to question the fact that she looks far better than the last time her saw her. If she is going to throw her problems in his face, he just wishes she'd go away.

Dawn grabs him by the shoulder and spins him on his chair to face her. Her standing, him sitting, their eyeballs are at exactly the same height. And, hmm, he thinks, she does look good.

"Well I guess I seek the Mighty Sardar then. I don't care what kind of circus you're running here but I'm on a mission. I need help. My sonuvabitch husband was your best friend. That sick bastard hurt my only daughter and left me to take the fall."

Burl. That's right, Sardar recalls, *that's the man that didn't kill me for sleeping with his daughter. We were best friends but that would have made it even worse...if he'd found out. Burl was not above killing someone.*

He also recalls the courtroom and Dawn standing there in front of the judge. It was so long ago. Maybe half a lifetime. Trying to maintain his composure Sardar replies, "I know. I was at the trial. I never understood why they convicted you."

"They railroaded me."

"They did," he says with resignation.

"Twenty-five years. I never heard from you."

"Frankly, I put that whole ugly mess behind me. You should too. I never saw Burl after that either."

"Here's the thing—I'm not so sure my daughter is

dead."

When the local police could not find the body of her missing daughter Kris, the whole town was convinced Dawn had murdered her. The jury followed suit. Sardar cleared out of the garage and that was that. Sardar needed to keep his hands clean. He never testified or ever gave it another thought one way or another but figured justice was done, even if he suspected Burl might have committed the murder himself. Still, the feelings came bubbling up like the trapped gasses in a swamp.

"Then where is she, Dawn? A phantom got her? You never explained yourself. Frankly, I'm not so sure you aren't trying to cover this up further."

"Maybe you never had faith in me. But I know in my heart-of-hearts that she's out there—somewhere, still breathing."

"Why are you so convinced?"

"The visions are coming to me."

"Mumbo-jumbo. If you are trying to out-psychic me, you've come to the wrong place."

"You're the only person that will believe. Maybe the only friend I have left."

"Friend?"

Cozying up to him seductively, she says, "You always had a soft spot for me. If we do this together, I'm confident we can find my daughter."

Sardar's voice rises. "So now you're out looking for the real killer? That's my problem? What's in it for me? What is it you think I owe you?"

A commotion outside interrupts their animosity-fest. Tires squeal. A siren wails, and police lights flood the room, drawing them to the window.

"Look at that," Sardar says. "I've never seen the police jump like that. They are really going after that old car."

"Better them than me."

"It looked like it was packed with girls."

Seizing the opportunity of the distraction, Dawn puts on the charm. She throws her arm around Sardar and snuggles close. "That siren scared me."

This time he does not brush her off. Yes, she does look good. "Oh don't worry," he says with confidence. "I got you."

The Mighty Sardar is back.

Chapter 3
The Garter Snakes Gang

Yes, out of Sardar's window, he can faintly discern a car full of girls and the police car completing a rubber-punishing U-turn in pursuit. Another sign that his life is about to change. And like everything else, he doesn't give it a second thought. He looks down at Dawn, who is shivering, and his mind goes to mush at the benefits of an inevitable hook-up.

The part that Sardar didn't see came twenty minutes earlier when a nasty piece of business took place.

The old car's occupants consisted of a group of girls calling themselves The Garter Snakes Gang, complete with their own gang colors, which was mostly a similar shade of green in their T-shirts. Lounging in the vicinity of a liquor store empty handed, the bunch was too young and too broke to buy anything. They just wanted to stick close to the juice.

Just when the girls thought there was no action to be had, enter petite Maris Plymouth, a flaxen haired socialite with a Daddy who had a thing for classic cars. Daddy collected them, jazzed up their innards, and then tossed Maris the ones he got bored with.

This night, daddy's little "ladybug" drove up in an Impala big enough to cause a gas shortage all on its own, and then sloppy-parked across two spaces with the intention of a quick stop to snap up the best vodka in stock.

When that extra-long door swung wide, the gang went all shifty-eyed, agog at her progress from the lot to the store, thirsting at her every move behind the plate glass window. Maris the silver-spooner was legendary in their town as someone who wanted for nothing.

"Ooh, she's going for the vodka. She'll buy enough mouthwash for all of us," gang member Nada boasted in her Russian tinged drawl, "if she knows what's good for her."

As Maris emerged with a bottle in hand, her furry Grucci purse rang out with the lyrics, "fly like a G6." With Maris going all arms and elbows to snatch out her bejeweled cell phone, the precious vodka bottle slipped from her grasp to smash on the ground. "Uh oh," she said.

In the eyes of the gang members, this tragedy all happened in Slo-Mo, every flying shard a bad dream, every glob of drink like a wet dollar sign made worthless on the walk.

Maris stamped her dainty foot, telling her caller, "Mom, see what you did? I think it splashed me! Definitely a couple of drops! I don't care what you called about, mom, I gotta go. I need more." Maris swiveled on her heels and returned through the glass door to get a replacement, grumbling, "So annoying!"

One particular gang girl, Nada, obviously with more acid in her stomach than the rest, let her jaw stick open at the sight.

Second-in-command Tamara went back to popping her gum as a provocative thought brought a wide smile to her ebony cheeks. "Hey, Nada, why don't you lap up that vodka doggie style?"

"Very funny, Tamara. After Perestroika, we stopped drinking out of puddles," the tall ex-wrestler replied. "There was no need to continue with American habits."

"Wrestle your ass back there if it was so great," Tamara laughed, "it'll be a Soviet reunion."

"Shut-up, you guys." Kris, the head honcho of the gang, said. "This is the time to nail that bitch."

No one responded.

"Unless you guys are chicken? And this ain't no henhouse under my command."

They all sized each other up, making a quick decision not to be hens. Five of them jumped into the car with their heads ducked while Nada, the strongest, remained standing by the hood.

When Maris once again emerged and headed for her car, Nada blocked her passage. "How about a lift," Nada said.

Maris was startled by the Russian's belligerent manner and thick accent, and the bottle again found its way to the pavement, this time splashing both of them. She said, "Nuts, now I have to go back again."

"You make me laugh, blondie." Nada said. "I was going to just take your car keys and let you go, but now you wasted another bottle of my favorite hot sauce and I'm looking forward to pummeling you." Nada spun Maris and fixed her in the crook of a half-Nelson. With her free hand, she reached into the heiress' purse and liberated her car keys, then shifted her prey behind the Impala's taillights. There, Nada landed her on the ground and rested a foot on her shoulder to signal her to stay quiet and not move. "Shhh!" Nada hissed. It was like catching a small lizard.

Nada tried the key in the trunk lock. No problem. When it sprung open, however, the edge delivered Nada the sort of hapless blow to the head that she'd suffered all too often in the ring. "Crap, another lump." She deposited Maris in the trunk and slammed it, just then thinking that the whole thing might have been done more discreetly, but she wasn't sure how.

All aboard, Kris commanded the wheel, and she pulled the old Chevy out in a hurry. After a brief drive, she selected a vacant lot. Nicely deserted, check! Daddy's Girl has got to go.

The gang piled out, fighting the moveable seats and each other to stand tall in their moment of infamy. They had graduated to bad ass car thieves and would need to get used to the idea. By the dim lights of the low beams, no one was talking.

"Now we've really done it," Red Herring, the youngest of the group, said boldly. "We got ourselves in deep."

"In deep, Red?" said Munzi, her fingertips massaging her temples under flowing black hair. "Sometimes I wish you'd stop watching episodes of *CSI Pipsqueak*, and shut your face. I'm trying to think."

"Well that will take forever," Kris said. "By then we'll have a dead body in the back."

"D-dead?" Red whimpered.

"Relax, pigeon." Munzi chortled.

"She won't be dead, but she'll wish she was," Patti said. It was an audacious statement from a nerdy girl with tape holding her glasses together and a retainer slurring her speech, especially on the W's.

"Alright, let's just do something. I have places to be!" Kris told them. This was her idea of motivation.

Nada threw the ball of keys to Kris. When the trunk lid opened, Maris was dazed and crying.

"Get ... the hell ... out!" Patti commanded. The others looked at each other, thinking this was overly harsh. Something about it coming from Patti didn't sit right.

Slowly, Maris unfolded herself, climbed onto the street and started finger combing her hair. Then she sort of cuddled her purse. For some unexplained reason, their prey was more interested in putting herself back together and comforting herself than trying to run.

Some of the girls giggled at the rich girl stroking her handbag as if it were a Chihuahua. This episode was a whole new level of amusement for the gang. Red couldn't help snickering too.

"Hmm," sadistic Patti said, rubbing her chin. "You think that's your doggie? Maybe you, my friend, are the doggie. Get down on all fours."

"That's original," said Kris.

"Pretty lady, huh?" Patti continued. "Nice pocketbook and everything."

Patti snatched the handbag from Maris and pulled out a lipstick. Unhinging the lid, Patti scribbled on Maris' face, all sloppy and downturned, making her look like a sad version of The Joker. "See how pretty you are now?"

"Well, I do have good genes. Thank you," Maris said, forgetting for a moment where she was and in whose company.

"Strip. Take everything off."

"Really, Patti?" said Munzi. She turned her back to

the action in an appeal to the others. "What are we running here? A lesbo-thon?"

That was when Patti spazzed back to her usual level. "It's for humiliation. Duh!"

"Yeah," Tamara backed her up. "Let's see rich girl's G-string. I bet it's gold-plated."

"I'm interested in how much gold she has in her purse," said Nada, who scooped it up.

"You're gonna add robbery to this, too?" Red complained.

Kris drew a line with her finger across her throat and Red knew what that meant. She didn't dare say anything else.

Maris dropped her clothes in a pile, one article at a time. And one by one, Red scarfed them up and threw the clothes into the open trunk. "I want those," she explained, warming to the idea of larceny when it came to designer floordrobe.

As clumsy Nada fumbled with the furry bag, the credit cards spilled out.

"Those will be too hot," warned Kris.

"Yeah, I know." Nada identified them and broke them one by one. "In my country, we don't have credit lines. We have bread lines."

Tamara found this very funny.

Maris took everything off except for her yellow and blue thong. She crossed her hands over her small breasts, protecting them from the chill air.

With an embarrassed nudge of encouragement from Red, Patti turned more sadistic. "You are so not finished, my dear."

On cue, Maris pulled her panties down, leaving her

with nothing but her designer high heels.

"I kind of like you like that," said Patti. "Keep the heels and the furry bag too."

As if she were a willing participant, Maris nodded and threw her panties to Red, who slipped them in her jacket pocket instead of the trunk.

"Seriously, we should get out of here before Patti asks for her tonsils," Kris advised them.

The six gang members all loaded into the Impala. Kris took the helm once more, fishtailing out of there, reminding the others why she didn't have a driver's license.

Chapter 4
The Getaway

Teen moptop Red Herring digs her fingers into the blue upholstery in front of her, mindless of what it is doing to the value of the mint 1967 Impala. After all, it isn't her car, nor can she expect much benefit of the spoils.

The Impala is less a car than a barge. Built twenty years before anyone bought a minivan, it is a true six-passenger sedan. Red, as the youngest and shortest of the crew, occupies the front hump seat – the space between the driver and coveted shotgun spot. Unlike the older, more confident girls on either side of her, or the three equally energized girls on the back bench, she is palpably scared. While the others are all smiling and laughing, Red's face is a pale, grimacing mask of remorse. Her companions don't understand. They do not even try to read the expression glaring back at them from the rearview mirror. Remorse like hers is something that faded from their own rear views years before.

Yes, she is a gang girl, but the youngest of them, and everything about tonight seems wrong. She doesn't want to look back. The trees, washed in police flashers, are screaming red and blue at her in the night. She and the other Garter Snakes have just stolen this gem of a car and the police are on them so fast that Red Herring wants to call it quits then and there. "Stealing clothes and stealing cars are two very different things." She directs her complaints to Kris, the fair-haired gang leader, who sits white-knuckled at the wheel.

If elder residents of town were there to notice it, it might register that teen Kris is the spitting image of Dawn's daughter— who was sacrificed to Kali. She has the same dirty-blond hair, round face and same rosy cheeks. But there's a difference: That other Kris would be forty years old by now. If she were alive.

Red says, "I am not a criminal. This is wrong. We really did a number on that girl."

This remark gets the unwanted attention of the brunette on the other side of Red.

With a tug at her studded denim vest, Munzi says, "Well I have no problem with it. What's your deal, Red Herring? You did it too." Munzi had learned to be a realist on the streets of Bensonhurst, Brooklyn.

Red Herring sulks. "I *said* 'we.'"

"Instant remorse doesn't make you blameless; it makes you a hypocrite."

"I know," said Red softly. The junior member could conveniently massage a fact or two when it suited her, and just as conveniently back off.

Tamara, Kris' second-in-command, leans forward from the back row and throws her hands in the air. "We got some respect is what happened!" Her halogen smile, like the bright headlamps of the vintage auto, takes some of the edge off her hard exterior. The rest of the gang cheers.

"She was really an innocent girl though," Red persists. "We should—"

"We should what?" Nada chimes in with an unmistakable eastern European accent. "We showed everyone how strong we are!"

Nada, a tall girl whose long legs are ill-suited to being a backseat passenger, pumps her arm in victory. In dissonance with her accent, she wears an Old Glory-pattern windbreaker over her mighty bicep. Had she been born into less austere circumstances, the toned, willowy raven-haired beauty might be a fashion model or a beach volleyball icon. But coming from a polluted, barely inhabitable end-of-the-railway-line town in central Russia, Nada's choices were limited. She had become a wrestler.

As if to confirm Nada's sentiments, the engine roars.

Red says, "Shouldn't we ... I don't know ... turn ourselves in?"

Kris, a tense dynamo at the wheel, informs her, "Are you out of your mind, Red? Me going to jail means you going six feet under!"

"Just kidding! Kidding." She says the words, but convinces no one.

The miles roll by, rural lanes fork, and red and blue lights fade. Kris checks the mirrors. "I think we lost them for now. I gotta turn somewhere before they see us again," she states calmly. Just then, she peers through the Impala's windshield toward the horizon. There's a street that I never seen before..."

"Turn, turn," Tamara urges from the back.

Kris pulls a right onto something that seems like a long private road. The headlights reveal a path through towering oaks that no longer sprout leaves on half their branches, their trunks choked in vines. Smaller elms are aligned in what were once hedgerows, but it is unlikely that gardener had seen this property in years. After a few beats, watching the overgrowth go by, it is Tamara who realizes this was no ordinary driveway. "Where are we?" she inquires, her dark visage equally capable of hiding mysteries as identifying them. "Whose place is this?"

Kris says, "Ours. At least for now it is."

She continues to drive up the path, slowly as to keep the Impala's V8 from rumbling any louder than an idle. Finally the Garter Snakes come to a broken down sign by the side of the road, and stop to inspect it by a busted lamp.

Red Herring takes the flashlight Munzi found in the glove box and shines it out the window. They see a single, horizontal, wooden plaque, its bright-yellow paint has mostly dissolved and the wood itself has been beaten by weather, nibbled by termites and cracked by tunneling worms. "Bonnie's B&B?" she reads, with a nervous upward inflection. "It's a bed and breakfast. I wonder if it's abandoned. I mean, that way we won't get in any more trouble."

In her intimidating Russian accent, Nada grunts, "Duh, chicken shit. Look at the sign. It's all rusted. Of course it's abandoned... Probably."

They continue down the road, slowing in a left turn hidden by an overgrown willow until they come to a long, low pre-fab that might have once been a pretty decent motel, now desolate and weather-beaten.

A sign to their right identifies BONNIE'S OFFICE. Red Herring wonders when was the last time a visitor checked in there.

Another sign says: MAIN HOUSE, and that one shows an arrow pointing across an open lawn fenced off like a grazing field for horses long gone. A pedestrian path crosses it and disappears into blackness.

Patti, the outlaw-nerd, is not very chatty – she is usually too preoccupied with her own thoughts to converse. When she does speak, it is often something profound. At this moment, she is moved to voice her observations, but all she can manage to say is, "Now this is creepy."

A curtain flutters in the office.

Nada asks, "Did I just see someone in the window?"

Munzi responds, "I did."

"It could be the trick of the light," says Patti.

Kris, whose job it is to stay tough, says, "I don't think so, but this spot is too weird and too cramped. We're going to the main house."

Tamara says, "I'll second that."

On the move again, they first re-trace their steps, and then find an offshoot road that leads where the sign had indicated. With only their headlights illuminating the shifting gravel, they negotiate a foliage-choked traffic circle and pull to a stop. The gang tumbles out of the car, each girl fighting for supremacy, but mostly anxious to see what they are getting into.

Red Herring feels snug in her leather jacket, her Garter Snakes symbol of inclusion. Even if they weren't in a place that inspires anxious chills, the late summer evening has a bite to it as if to warn that the frosty season that Massachusetts politely calls autumn means to take over all at once.

Kris, Patti, Red, Nada, Tamara, and Munzi form a line, shoulder-to-shoulder, across the driveway and stare in awe at the enormity of the place. The building rises stark white in the headlights they left on, its black shutters lending a sinister edge. The central block is massive; even at two stories tall, it can still properly be called a mansion given the way it expands to a maze of tree-shrouded side wings that fade into the night. They are only seeing a fraction of the behemoth.

The first four girls across the line, starting from Kris, help express the single thought they all seem to share telepathically.

"Ho—."

"—ly."

"Shit."

"Man."

Tamara adds, "Bonnie's is bed, breakfast, lunch *and* dinner."

Munzi, dismissive, breaks the spell. "No wonder the fuckers went out of business. Who could fill this place?"

Kris, ever practical, says, "The most important thing now is how do we bust in there."

Red Herring looks at her aghast. "So we're breaking and entering, too?"

Nada gives Red a shove. "Red, make yourself useful. See if the door is open. It's freezing."

As Red Herring walks up and tries the door, the rest crowd the landing behind her. They are sheltered by an overhang as a light rain – not hard, not heavy, just enough to combine with the cold to make everyone miserable – begins to splash off the Impala and worm into the butterfly windows Kris left open.

"It's locked," whines Red, "which means we're not welcome."

That answer satisfies none of her fellow Garter Snakes.

Nada, giving the knob a second go, opines, "No it isn't. It's just stuck." She raises a muscular leg and lands a sloppy kick in the center of the heavy door. Nothing gives. In embarrassment, she says, "If I had an ax I could unstick it."

Munzi twists the knob, bumps at the door with her shoulder, and thumps it with the bottom of her fist.

Patti cocks her head to one side pensively and says, "First thing tomorrow, I'm going to learn to pick locks."

Tamara throws up her hands. "That's it. I'm gettin' the crowbar." She starts back to the car, but Kris stops her.

"Wait, lemme see."

The gang leader cracks her knuckles, lays her hand on the knob, gives it a turn...

... and it just opens for her, flying back at high speed without a push until it bangs the wall behind it and doesn't bounce.

Patti screams, thinking she sees a blue phantom bustling out the door. Once it clears out she says, "That should not have just happened!" If anyone else saw the ghostly shape too, no one ventures to comment on it.

Kris pauses to absorb the whole phenomenon, but quickly recovers her mantle of leadership. "Well okay. See that? The house knows I'm in charge."

Patti lends an anxious voice to the unease they all feel. "I think we'll be safer in the car."

"Yes," Red chimes in quickly. "I'm with Patti."

Kris, though, has made up her mind. "No. Everybody goes in."

As they filter in, the girls fumble around in the dark entranceway somehow bumping into each other in the wide open space.

Kris grumbles, "I can't see a thing."

"Where are the damn lights?" Munzi asks. "None of these switches work."

"Maybe the bulbs are dead," says Tamara.

"There has to be a circuit breaker somewhere," offers Patti in pensive speculation.

"Hah!" Nada challenges. "You want to be the one to find your way to the basement?"

"God of Power… Let there be fluorescence!" Red Herring claps her hands twice, in mock imitation of a late-night TV commercial. At that, the gang hears a rising industrial-sized hum. The hallway chandelier blinks a few times, then holds steady.

Munzi says, "Holy crap, Red. How'd you do that?"

Chapter 5
Some Ground Rules

Having lit up the house like a magician, Red can't sort out her own feelings—happy and scared?—much less explain them to the other girls. "I don't know what I did. I was just goofing around."

Patti chews her lip. "Interesting that the generator is still working."

Red Herring says, "I hope no one's here."

"There had better not be," says Nada, addressing at a theatrical volume those to whom the warning would apply. "They'll escape out the back if they know what's good for them."

"Look at this place," says Tamara, absorbing the odd architecture and décor. Some sick taxidermist has stuffed and mounted animals not in their majestic, pristine state, but in the pangs of their death throes. The animals – large game, small game, domesticated pets – glare down at the gang from perches at all levels on the walls. Larger-than-life effigies of gods unknown west of the Ganges peer out from nooks that seem to have no other purpose but to serve as discreet altars to them. "What a crazy house. Who builds a thing like this?"

Red Herring mutters, "Yeah, weird."

"Down here," calls their leader.

They proceed along the hallway at Kris's lead.

Munzi, fumbling with her cheap, disposable, talk-and-text phone, says, "My cell's not working. Oh, there it is… Gone again."

"What do you even want your cell for?" Kris demands.

Munzi says," I'm trying to order a pizza."

"Real funny, dumbass. I found a room. Get in there."

They all file into the room on their right. The spacious area stands in stark contrast to the passageways leading to it. It is a perfectly hospitable hearth room, with porcelain and wicker knickknacks on the mantle, a thick-padded Persian rug underfoot, and a comfy, floral-patterned couch with white lace protectors still pinned neatly to the fabric. The walls are a soothing ochre trimmed softly with eggshell white. There are no books in the recessed bookcases and no pictures up on the walls, but it seems that whoever abandoned the place did so recently and not in too much of a hurry.

The girls kick back and relax for the first time since stealing the Impala – a bare 20 minutes ago, but they all would have guessed it had been a matter of hours. They remove their jackets and are revealed in the Garter Snakes' gang-sign green T-shirts. They all wear blue or black jeans except for Patti, who breaks the dress code with a mid-length denim skirt instead. Kris also wears a red serpent necklace very much like the one that earlier Kris wore the day she died.

Patti says, "I'm exhausted."

Red Herring adds, "I have to find a bathroom. I need to pee."

Hold it," Kris barks. "No one goes anywhere until I lay down some rules."

"What rules?" Tamara asks warily. Her words convey an innocent question, but her body language – standing sideways in relation to Kris, providing the smallest target – belies her suspicion of the gang's leader. Tamara has a secret she intends to keep from Kris, but that's not the reason for her unease. Truth is, she isn't sure why she's so anxious around Kris at this moment. Tamara had noticed before, on fleeting occasions, that the planes and angles of Kris' unique face could sometimes look very different when she turned one way or another. This particular angle seemed disturbingly transformative. Tamara gets that impression very strongly right now, and looks around at the rest of the Garter Snakes. If there's something peculiar about Kris, they haven't picked up on it yet. Maybe, Tamara supposes, it's just her own hormones playing tricks.

"There's probably all kinds of good shit in here," Kris begins. "I'm talking about how we divide it up."

Tamara broods. "Is that all you think about, Kris?"

Red Herring, sounding a little too innocent and excited for a young woman most of the way through high school, offers hopefully, "We're like pirates."

"Yes," Kris says, stretching the word into a hiss. "We're like pirates if that helps you."

Nada says, "I say we divide it up by whoever can lift the most."

"You would want that, Rocky IV," says Munzi, doing some shadow boxing and sound effects.

"Ivan Drago," Nada corrects, supplying the Russian character's proper name while giving Munzi's pony tail a good yank.

"Yeah, whatever."

Kris ignores them. "If you find money, no one touches it until I see it. Jewelry and small objects, same thing. I *will* check your pockets. Well, that's really the only rule."

Red Herring raises her hand like she is still in school. "Kris?"

"Yes, Red. Go pee."

"Is anyone going with me?"

"Go. Pee," Kris meters out from her last nerve.

Chapter 6
Emergence

Red remembers how Kris was the first time she appeared in her high school. Bookless, friendless, confused. She was thinking of saying something to the newcomer when Candy Traynor came up to Kris. Candy...the senior terror who liked to say to Red, "the color of your hair makes me ill. Don't be surprised if I pull it all out one day."

Kris was just watching the river of people pass her station, and Candy said to her, "If you're training to be a statue, new girl, you must enjoy being covered in poop."

Without a rejoinder, Kris just punched her in the face, knocked her right to the floor. Everyone was so shocked that Red was the only one to applaud. But then Kris just went back to staring blankly.

Red came up to her and said, "What's your name?"

"Kristine."

"You go to school here?"

"For now I do."

Looking at Candy on the floor and the other kids clearing out fast, Red asked, "Think she'll ever wake up?"

"Who cares?"

"If you still want to go to this school tomorrow, I'd better get you out of here."

Kris examined her with muddled curiosity. "You're an annoying girl with a whiny voice. Are we friends?"

Jumping at the opportunity, Red cheered, "Yes!"

And just then, Tamara spoiled their moment when

she ran down the hallway, kicked the unconscious Candy in the side, and ran on.

"Good," said Kris, confirming her friendship with Red, but pointing after Tamara. "Then you can introduce me to her."

That was how Tamara became second-in-command, and Red's stock just kept plummeting from there.

Chapter 7
Nerd Enthusiasm

Tracing her steps back to a powder room she noticed on the way in, Red Herring can't stop shaking. She wishes she had never taken off her jacket, although it is dubious that the cold is the only reason for her trembles. Hands quivering, she fumbles with the knob as she closes and locks the door. Rain – harder now – batters against the tiny window.

These are not the most sanitary conditions under which she has ever relieved herself. There are skid marks in the bowl, puddle marks on the seat and floor. The plunger looks like it needs its own plunger. A persistent stench emanates from molds that formed on the human detritus as well as on the organic material in the caulk. Rusty pipes leak little rivulets that slowly rot the floorboards under the tile. Judging by the way the white ceiling paint sags in a big bubble in the middle of the room, something similar is going on upstairs.

There is nowhere near enough toilet paper – just the last few squares of a roll that had been left behind – just lying on the floor, not even on a spool. Red decides to invest all but the last half dozen squares in covering every inch of the toilet seat.

Dropping her pants to her feet, she settles in and tries to concentrate on the task at hand. But weird sounds surround her like muttering, incoherent voices blending into the splatter of the rain beyond the windows.

"Kris?..." she tries first.

Then "Nada?...

Munzi?...

Patti?"

No answer but those warped noises proceeding unabated. Apparently, none of the gang members are there testing her. The overlapping susurrations are something else.

After a few more moments of pent up anxiety, she rises from the sticky seat and does a dropped-pants walk around the bathroom. Her hand, mummied-up with the remaining toilet paper, hangs at her side, a short train of two-ply.

Red makes her way to the corner where she had seen a broomstick. Harassed by the voices at every turn, she doesn't notice that the broomstick has acquired company. Her head swivels back and forth between the source of the sound and the general direction of the stick. But after several awkward paces, her peripheral vision is good enough to allow her to wrap her hand around her potential wooden savior and she begins to move it across to defend herself.

With her grip firm, she suddenly realizes that the stick is rippling with the movement of badly disturbed freakishly giant locusts. These are not any kind of locusts she has seen before. They have the same body shape and wing span, and on top of that, too many legs – horrible, spindly, needle-like legs.

Now these spider-locusts leap off in all directions. One lands on her bare thigh. "Shit, shit, shit, shit, shit, shit, shit!" Red wallows in disgust, wailing at so high a pitch it barely registers as speech.

The sound of Red Herring's annoying squeal echoes through the house, but the other girls shrug it off instead of coming to her aid. They are busy re-enacting their crime from earlier in the night.

"There are times when you are hot, and we were hot!" yells Kris. "Right girls?"

Munzi nods. "We were hotter."

Brimming with nerd enthusiasm, Patti beams, "We were kicking ass and writing checks we couldn't cash."

Kris shakes her head. "That makes no sense, Patti."

Munzi gloats, "The minute I set eyes on that car, I knew we were going for a joy ride."

Stepping in front, Tamara says, "That bitch got in the way of our fun."

"And she got it good," Kris confirms.

"No one messes with the Garter Snakes," says Nada.

At her invitation, they collectively touch fingers and hiss, their gang sign.

Miming a driver at the wheel, Munzi recounts, "She pulled up to the stoplight. Remember? And she said, 'Hey, I'm looking for trouble.'"

Tamara steps in again. "Naw. She said, 'You ladies want my car?'"

They giggle.

Munzi continues, "And then she said, "Here's the keys, Tamara. And let's French kiss to seal the deal."

The girls cackle as Munzi mimes a tonsil-rattler with her swishing tongue.

"The kiss-of-death," adds Tamara. "I'm the one who took charge."

"*I* gave the order for you to take charge," Kris reminds her pointedly.

Smacking her palm with a callused fist, Nada says, "And that's where I came in to knock her block off."

Kris says, "Yeah, after I gave the order, you pulled her out of that driver seat so fast and threw her on the ground like the piece of trash she is. Wise-off to us, huh?"

They agree.

"And can't I take any credit here?" Patti asks. "I looked in the glove compartment to see if she owned the car, to make sure we could rightfully steal it from her."

"Then I slammed her face into the curb," Munzi chimes in.

"Because I said so," Kris reminds her. "And since Red Herring is in the crapper, let's pretend Patti was our victim."

Patti shakes her head no, but Nada snatches her up.

Munzi says, "I gave her a right-hook like this." She mock-hits Patti.

"And a punch to the ol' bread box," says Tamara, poking Patti in the stomach.

"Stop it, you guys. Get off."

Patti stumbles forward as they release her.

Nada says, "You could never be a wrestler, Patti. Pathetic."

Patti, in her toughest voice, says, "I'm no victim. I do the harm. I told that bitch to strip down to her undies, right then and there."

"Yeah," Kris muses, "That was mean and fucked-up."

Nada asks, "Why'd you do that?

51

"She *should* be disgraced," says Patti. "After talking to us like that? She took off her shirt, and I said 'That's not good enough.' She took off her bra. Still not good enough. Everything off!"

Red Herring has re-entered the room irritated by their exaggerations, but holds her tongue a little longer.

Patti crows, "I made the bitch walk home naked."

"And we took her sweet ride," Kris finishes.

Red Herring pushes into the middle of them, oblivious of her low status – so new she doesn't even know to act like the new girl. "That's not how it happened. She was in the liquor store and left the keys in the car. You humiliated her for no reason. You *had* the car..."

Salvaging what she can, Patti says, "But she did go home butt naked. All right, losers, I'm going to bed."

Kris says, "Real exciting, Patti."

None of them think about their rich victim Maris, who has not been to bed yet either. She traces a path along the road from the wide spot where they'd left her.

"Anyyyybody out there!!!!!????" she cries.

Speaking to her furry handbag, she says, "Wilky, I'm sorry! If I hadn't taken daddy's vintage car for a secret beer run, this wouldn't have happened. Someone has to come by to help us if we wait here, right? I can entertain you meanwhile. Wanna hear a joke, Wilky? All right then. A rich blond girl gets her car stolen. She calls the police on her cell phone. Two cops pull up to find her stark naked with a hot dog.

"The first cop says, 'what happened to your clothes?'

"The rich blond says, 'I gave the robbers the outfit to match the upholstery.'

"The second cop says, 'What were you going to do standing there naked with the hot dog?'

"The girl shrugs and says, 'I didn't know you were going to get here so soon.'"

She giggles at the risqué finale. Wilky the handbag is unimpressed.

Apparently responding to some snide remark from her companion, Maris shouts, "Well what's your point exactly? ...we might just make it, Wilky, did that ever cross your designer-label brain? ...Well regardless, I would rather take my chances out there on the road back to my house than to stay here and die on this shithole parking lot, spending the rest of my life talking to a goddamn furry handbag!"

Maris reaches into the handbag in question, takes out a handkerchief, and blows her nose with a nice solid honk.

Not five minutes after her announcement about sacking out, Patti finds the nearest boudoir, chucks her glasses on the nightstand and sprawls out in the king-sized bed in groggy bliss. The room is classic B&B, very nicely appointed, but with odd angles foreign to our more-standardized, prefabricated times. Ignoring the irrational sense of wrongness creeping up and down her spinal cord, she convinces her higher brain that she has discovered a perfectly safe place. The rain, tapering off now, lulls her to a sleep so solid it's like she's knocked cold.

Tamara slips quietly into the room, tiptoes across,

and eases into the bed, way too close to Patti. "Oooh, little Patti sleeping there just like my baby in my womb," Tamara whispers, careful not to wake the fitfully dozing beauty nerd.

Patting her own belly for a moment, Tamara nestles in softly and cradles Patti's head in her arms, making Patti a stand-in her future baby.

"You gonna be my little Garter Snake? Huh, baby snake? You gonna be the newest little Garter Snake in the gang? When you pop out of me, babe, it's gonna be sweet. Let me tuck you in."

Tamara pulls the covers higher for the sleeping Patti. "Aww. You're so cute, don't want you to catch cold now. Nothing is too good for my sweet angel. Baby food? No real food." Breaking out the baby-talk, she says, "Oh, you wany something else? I see. You look thirsty. Yes you do. You had a big day."

Rocking her fellow gang member, who is now somehow something more to her, Tamara says, "I'll prove to my mother that she hasn't looked at me in nine damn months, right baby? Aww, I forgot, you're still thirsty. That's right. Mama's gonna feed you now. Get ready. Here comes the good stuff. Vitamin D straight from the tap."

She opens her shirt part way, and squeezes out her breast. "But you gotta be good. Say 'mama,' sweetheart, 'mama,' and clamp hold right here."

Tamara swipes her nipple against Patti's lips back and forth a few times until it parts them. "Suck your fill, baby. Go on."

This continues for many long seconds with Tamara rubbing at Patti's lips every which way and urging her ample breast forward.

Patti actually begins to make a suckling motion just before she awakens, beyond startled, flying back. "W-W-What is this?"

"What's the matter?"

"What do you mean 'what's the matter!?' What the hell, Tamara?"

"I was practicing breast feeding."

"On me?" Patti yells, rubbing her mouth. "That's so weird and twisted. And creepy. And random."

"Really, Patti? How can you say that? How can you sit there and say that? Is it weird and twisted to learn to take care of my baby? Creepy? It's natural. Random? It's my baby... it's popping out of me like it or not... I need to know what it's like. Right now." She strikes the recalcitrant Patti on the back with a pillow to make her point.

"Not on me. Get a doll or something. This is fucking Freudian. I feel grossed-out that I was a part of your messed up, parental complex."

"It was nothing," Tamara shrugs. "No harm done."

"Nothing? You just shoved your tit in my mouth!"

"It happens every day."

"Not to me!"

"Patti, you of all people should know, that if any of us had been breast fed, we wouldn't have turned out like this. We are the Garter Snakes, right? United?"

Tamara holds her finger out to do the gang sign hiss but Patti doesn't budge.

"Get... the hell... out!"

Tamara goes, but the damage was done. Just then,

Nada calls out from the hallway, "Tamara! Patti!"

"Great," says Patti, throwing her hands in the air. "Now I'm awake."

Chapter 8
Skull Fuckers

The girls, all of them, clunk down a long, creaky set of stairs. The risers are soft with mold and warped with moisture. Wood splinters but doesn't quite shatter under heavy boot heels. At the bottom of the basement staircase is a boiler room, the picture of squalor. There are so many piles of debris the space could hide anything.

Nada says cheerfully, "Our next order of business is to find the vodka. Should be down here somewhere..."

Kris lilts, "That gets my blessing."

Red Herring brightens. "My first real drink!"

Kris turns to Red. "Who said you're getting any?"

"She never gets any," Munzi quips.

"This basement is the freakiest thing I've ever seen," Patti informs them with her usual solemnity.

Kris says, "It's going to get a whole lot freakier if I don't find some al-co-hol!"

"I'm just saying," Patti murmurs in her defense as she backs away from Kris and brushes up against Munzi.

"Get off me, Lezzie."

"But I didn't do anything."

"And when I get drunk," says Munzi, "see that it stays that way. Don't take advantage. I ain't that kind a girl."

Nada says, "Sure, Munzi, and I promise I won't mention senior year and your experimentation." She sets that last word in air quotes.

"Cut it, bitch," Munzi warns.

"Guys," says Red Herring, "all this stuff we're doing will just make us worse off when they catch us."

Kris rounds on her. "You can cut it, too, traitor. That's all we got around here—weirdos, faggots and squealers."

Over her shoulder, Tamara says, "Where do you fit in that mix, Kris?" Right on top of her remark, Tamara lets out a startled shout as a wooden board falls away to reveal a skull. It's human and it's a real one. "What is a skull doing down here?" Tamara asks everybody and nobody. "You think some kind of supernatural cult got into this place? What if the skullfuckers are still in here?"

Kris says, "That's great, Tamara. Here we go with your supernatural crap."

Patti can't hold in her ire anymore. "Tamara— you want something spooky?— Why don't you go have an alien baby?"

Tamara twitches with a startle. "How dare you tell everyone here that I'm knocked up?"

"Listen bitch," says an unrelenting Patti, "After you pretended to breast-feed me while I was asleep, you expect me to keep a secret?"

The girls collectively let out an "ew, gross" like some sort of teen Greek chorus.

"Preggers?" asks Kris. There is a moment when all else fades away, the dessicated B&B, the carjacking, the Garter Snakes gang – and there are just two young women, Kris and Tamara, friends and confidants who have yet to go down the path that brought them to this moment.

Still, that was so three-months-ago. To Tamara's chagrin, Kris's mask of concern turns to a fit of derisive laughter.

"That makes you a bitch-and-a-half!" Kris jests sophomorically between guffaws. She points at Tamara's face. "Bitch—" And then at her stomach. "And a half. Get it?" she laughs again. Nobody else thinks it's funny. The gang, who had been standing around in a circle during this breach of confidence, splinters off to look for valuables.

Tears spring to Tamara's eyes, but there is more fierceness than sadness in the penetrating, dark brown orbs. "That was a secret!"

"Shut up, you whores!" says Patti, who has gravitated toward some promising-looking cabinetry. "I just found the good stuff. Let's drink up." She gives a little victory dance.

They each grab two bottles and begin to carry their bounty up from the basement when Nada notices something odd about the bottles in her hands. "This is not vodka."

Patti reports, "There's no labels on them at all. Bathtub gin... er, wine. Or something. How do we know what we're drinking?

"It's liquor," barks Kris. "Drink it or I will."

Where did the time go? That's what the Garter Snakes gang wants to know as it seems like the sun will never come up. The party is endless. What was in those bottles? It's long gone, but it was surely not vodka or anything else brewed on this good earth.

Kris is more inebriated than anyone else. She is known to crack awful jokes when she drunk and this night is no exception. "What do you call a nun with her period?'

Munzi pops up from the floor. "Huh?"

"Mother bloody Mary."

Munzi hits the floor with a thump. "Ow."

In a flash of pure inspiration, Patti says, "Let's get outta here! This party blows!"

All agree. "Red!" commands Kris. "Open us the door."

Red goes to the nearest outside door and puts her hand on it. She gets no traction. "No good. The grab thing is slippery. It keeps getting away from me," she laughs.

"Give it to me," says Munzi. "Hand it to me, I'll try it. I'll try anything."

"My water broke!" Tamara says.

"That's the fire water, you clumsy *duna*," Nada says.

They are silent for a mere second and it's too much to bear. Kris says, "Let's put some music on," as she flips on what looks like a radio from the golden age. The back is off so the when the tubes glow, the light adds an eerie illumination to the room. After a burst of static, and some variable frequency whistling, the radio announcer comes on and proclaims, "K.A.L.I. is on the air!" What follows are tribal drums and modern rock guitar in a combination never before heard on Earth. The girls sway to the beat.

"That is what I'm talking about," says Tamara. "Solid gold!"

As if on cue, the gang jumps to their feet – suddenly infused with energy – to get a piece of the booming beat in whatever interpretive way they see fit. Munzi grabs Patti like a rag doll. She grinds her crotch into Patti's, while pushing up her palms to raise the roof. The other girls are too bombed out to notice the amorous nature of their encounter, faux or not. Nada shadow-boxes in the corner and Red plays air guitar. Kris sticks out her long tongue and winds it in a windmill like a possessed Miley Cyrus, cheering on the festivities with an incomprehensible dentist's office moan.

"The drums!" Kris screams. "The drums are in me."

That's when the house disappears leaving only a feeling of wet grass and slippery snake skin.

"I feel real funny," Nada says. "Is this the American dream?"

But it is not a dream. It is a full-on nightmare. The walls come back and bleed colors out of a psychedelic hallucination.

Now most of the group lines up on the dirty basement floor, thinking they are on some kind of slip-slide ride at a water park. They wriggle like fish until they are exhausted by orgiastic pleasure. Kris bops and boogies around them in a frenzy.

What was in those bottles?

Chapter 9
Slimebag

Finally daybreak. Adequately sober, Munzi slips away from their basement playground to find some privacy upstairs.

She eases her cellphone out of her pocket, and paces around as she texts. In public, Munzi is the most self-possessed of the gang. Privately, she has always been a bundle of nerves. She fidgets from her fingers to her restless legs. Her expressive face, which easily contorts to whatever mood the situation calls for, crinkles into a tooth-grinding visage of anxiety. Her eyes dart about the room, seeing everything and looking at nothing, as she taps out the text by sure-handed feel.

She stops, reads it back, plays with the furniture and various knickknacks. If this works, finally they'll get some damn pizza in here. Hopefully someone has money to pay for it. Nada creeps in behind her, clad now in a blue security guard shirt. Munzi doesn't see her. Anywhere else and the streetwise Munzi would have sensed a threatening presence over her shoulder, but since entering the house, she has been bombarded with enough tingles of suspicion that she has come to tune them out.

Patiently, Nada waits for the right moment to lunge.

Suddenly, Munzi stops her constant motion. She stands still, her phone taking all her attention as she awaits confirmation that her *send* command has been accepted. With Munzi's back fully turned, Nada pounces on her as easily as a leopard lands on a gazelle, throws her down, knee in her back like a crowd control cop taking down a rioter, and pins her arms as if she were going to slap on handcuffs and beat her LA-style.

Nada's thick accent gives way to a cop-show character voice as she yells: "Freeze! You're under arrest, slimebag!" The handcuffs are fake rubber ones that she slips onto the prone girl.

Munzi, always so tough, starts to cry. "I didn't do anything!" she pleads. "My phone is right over there. I wanna call my mom. Get off! You're hurting me!"

Nada keeps the pressure on for only a moment, but far too long for a prank from Munzi's perspective.

"I'll get off all right," Nada says, dissolving back into her natural voice and accent. "I'll get off on a sense of authority."

"Nada? You jackass."

Reluctantly flipping the hapless Munzi right side up, Nada says, "Come on, guidette. Play along. This is bonding..."

"Bonding?"

"I mean bondage. The S and the M."

Shedding the rubber manacles, Munzi says, "Shit, Nada, I don't find it funny. You know I hate handcuffs."

"Suit yourself. You are funny you Americans. You break too easy. In my country, we don't crap in our panties."

"Where did you get that uniform?"

"I found this shirt in the closet, and from then on, the joke was on you. I do shit like this whenever I get drunk. It could have been much, much worse. You cried like a baby. The rest is history. We had the cold war, but you hit the cold floor." She laughs, thinking that a clever rhyme, and then she adds uselessly, "I'm so drunk."

"Well watch yourself next time, you big gorilla. Or..."

"Or what? Americans are so weak."

Nada falls down laughing, "Who were you texting anyway?" Before she can get an answer, she passes out.

Chapter 10
Not as You Imagine

Fortunately for him, Gary Sardar does not have to rely on his income as a showman. Those who make their money in securities markets are often called "gurus" or "swamis." The appellation is intended ironically, but is occasionally the literal truth. Whether this "investi-digitation" is done with quantitative modeling or intuition or what is ascribed to "luck," it requires a sensitivity to vibrations in nature that most do not feel. It was this sensitivity that paid for his neatly kept Colonial in historic Marblehead. Dawn is duly impressed with the splendor, giggling like a girl.

The Mighty Sardar has now taken the tour to his bedroom, Heaven-sent or Hell-bent on recreating the sort of relationship that he had with her daughter. She is giving him every encouragement.

"I hope you didn't leave all your turbans at the office," says Dawn.

The remark gives him pause. Does she know what he and Kris did all those years ago? He wasn't anywhere near discreet, now that he comes to think of it.

"For protection," she explains.

"Protection? I'm nowhere near that big."

"Oh it's not a real turban. You hide things in there. If a joint, why not a condom?"

"Oh. Uh-oh. You do know."

"Don't worry. I love the idea of being with the same

man my daughter was with."

"I am not sure this is the best idea I ever had," says Sardar, but as usual, he does it anyway.

Morning finds Sardar in a white, fresh-out-of-the-bag crewneck T-shirt and plaid pajama bottoms out of the L.L. Bean catalog. Across the breakfast nook table, Dawn, who has slept in, settles into a seat wearing his rust-orange Brooks Brothers robe. It is so big on her that its hem drags on the ground, yet so low-cut in front that her breasts freely tumble out.

Pouring the coffee and stretching like a lioness, she says, "I feel good as new. Sorry I came on so strong last night, but I was in jail a long time."

Looking up from his newspaper, Sardar says caustically, "I hope I was as good in bed as your ex-husband Burl. He told me some things. He said he did all that kinky stuff with you."

"Yeah, Burl was into some crazy shit. None of it good. Could you please not bring that up? I'm with you now."

"And I thank you for that," he says, framed by kitchen wallpaper of crosshatched vines. His post-orgasm brain kicks in. "So when will you be leaving?"

This is the moment Dawn realizes that last night meant something different to each conjugal partner. To Dawn, it was a necessary part of a plan to entice the showman into caring enough to risk his own safety on her behalf. Some women can do that without any emotional investment, but she is not wired that way. She cannot manipulate a man without manipulating herself. She has contorted herself emotionally to the point where she is giddily in love with this man. To Sardar, though, it was simply bonus sex thrown his direction. Dawn's jaw drops in what she perceives to be betrayal. "Leaving?"

"You have a ... third of your life ahead of you," Sardar explains, exercising one of his rather inept attempts at kindness. "I have to get back to the club to check inventory."

"You haven't seen me in twenty-five years and you're kicking me out?"

"I'm not your husband. I'm not your boyfriend. I don't know what you want from me."

"Don't give me that," Dawn fires back. "I still need your help finding my kid. I already put up collateral."

The word hangs in the air. Saying it makes her realize the truth underlying her own emotional state.

"That's what last night was?" Sardar asks, but he asks on both their behalves. "Collateral?"

Sobbing a little, she says, "How else would you come to the aid of an ex-con?"

She always knew Sardar's weakness for weepy women. He says, "Don't cry, Dawn." Confused now, he adds, "I don't understand something. You must be about fifty-five."

"Yes," she demands. "So what?"

"Oh no, no. You look very young, but your daughter must be close to forty," Sardar says. He looks her up and down and realizes how truly he speaks. Dawn's face is unlined. Her breasts are still taut and perky. In fact, she almost reminds Sardar not so much of how she looked a quarter century earlier, but how her *daughter* looked back then. "Kris couldn't possibly have been held captive for twenty-five years. Her body was never found by the police."

"That's my point. Her body was never found."

"After all this time, you must let hope die."

On the offensive now, Dawn says, "You're all right with this? Your buddy Burl worshiped Kali, an ancient Indian power. He didn't just dabble in the dark arts. He went all the way. And when he needed a virgin sacrifice, he chose his disobedient daughter."

Retreating into his newspaper and coffee, Sardar says, "Sacrifice? Burl? I knew him a long time. He was capable of a lot of things, but not atrocities. And if he did anything, I didn't know about it."

"Well you should have known. You were tight with Burl. Are you saying he planned a murder and told you nothing?"

Taking another tack, Sardar says, "Maybe he didn't kill her, and … she's out there somewhere. You could be right about that. But I still need proof. Things are rarely as you imagine them to be."

To make his point, Sardar surprises Dawn with a trick he could practically do in his sleep, setting off a flash of fire and smoke in his hand. He never breaks eye contact even as the white flare of incinerating celluloid explodes out of his palm. Dawn gasps and recoils from the table.

Chapter 11
Busted Tomato

Kris is first to awaken after a night of intense dreams that cannot be entirely attributed to ethyl alcohol. All the Garter Snakes are sleeping on or adjacent to the comfy couch. Munzi and Nada have found their way back to the group and flopped down with them, taken by a psychic aftershock. Now it's hangover time. Kris bats away the collection of arms and legs draped over her.

"My head feels like a busted tomato," Kris moans with uncharacteristic candor.

The rest of the girls stir and wake one at a time. Kris can tell at a glance they all feel as crappy as she does. Not that they count that much.

Forgetting her place as the second in command, Tamara says, "Keep it down to a whisper."

"I'll keep *you* down to a whimper."

Patti pops up with a start. "How did my pants get wet?"

The girls snicker. "Patti wet her pants," teases one of the girls in a falsetto. Patti looks around, but cannot identify which of her companions was mocking her. It doesn't really matter.

Rising off the throw pillow on the floor, which sufficed as her mattress, she sniffs, detects no odor from urine. "It's from the wine, you jerks!"

Nada sits up causing her head to bump off the arm of the couch. "Let's clear the fuck out of here. The cops are probably long gone."

They all pick themselves up and move, filing toward the front door like good little girls tamed by the stifling hangovers.

As Munzi puts her hand on the doorknob, however, Kris is seized by a moment of panic.

"Hold up. What do you want to do? Lead the lives of upstanding citizens? We can't go back. Not ever."

Bullshit," Munzi shoots back. "Nobody got killed. One girl got beaten and stripped. One car got borrowed. I for one would like to not die in here like a rat."

Kris regards her for a moment as if persuaded by that wisdom. She backs off and allows Munzi to try the door.

Munzi goes at it with a twist and then a frustrated yank. It's sealed.

Tamara takes her own go at it, making sure the top and bottom bolts aren't holding it in place. They aren't. "Shit."

It doesn't even cooperate with Kris this time. She says, "It's the same trouble we had on the way in. Worse."

"The door can't stay locked from both sides," Patti reckons.

Tamara says, "Well, it is anyway."

Patti taps her lips in concentration. "This isn't the door we came in. That one opened before. So that's the way out."

They cross back to the door they entered from, only to find Door Number One equally solid and impassible. But then they follow Tamara's gaze to the window. "Who needs a door when the place is loaded with bustable glass?"

Swinging a croquet mallet, Nada says, "I got

something for that. I found it in the basement." With a big splayed hand, she warns them, "Stand back."

The big Russian goes up to the window, takes off her jacket, and balls it up to cover her face up to the eyes. With her free hand, she swings the mallet down at the window. Before it reaches the glass, it glances off an invisible force field with an ominous, resounding thump. The backlash from her stroke comes right at her head and connects with a sickening thud.

Throwing the mallet away, she yells, "Aw, fuck. That hurts." She swipes at a lump rising over her eye.

Munzi cries out, "What the hell just happened?"

Inquisitive Patti reaches with tentative care to examine the vicinity of the window from the panes to its casing. "It's cold here," Patti observes. When she gets close, the air itself curves in a multi-colored warp that throws off a crackle and hum. "An invisible barrier! We can't get near it." Running her hands as close as the bend in reality allows, she whispers, "I wonder if they're all like that."

The girls instinctively back away from the windows, retreating to the grand staircase in the expansive foyer.

Rubbing her head, Nada says, "I don't care what anyone says. I'm not gonna try that again."

Kris rounds on Red Herring. "Red, you the one locked us in here, aren't you?"

Red shies from the accusation. "No." Kris has done nothing threatening to Red except to get into her personal space. Still, Red cannot help hunching her shoulders and backing up against the wall.

"Yeah you did." In a mocking and overly whiny

approximation of Red Herring, she whimpers, "Let's give ourselves up, don't break the door, don't steal the hooch, nahh, waaa—"

"That's not what I sound like."

"Yeah you do, traitor. So now you have us on lock down until the cops show up, huh? Like that incantation and hand clap trick, only I can't figure out how you did it."

"What's the matter with everyone?" Red yelps, swinging her arms wide. Her fingers graze Kris' cheek.

Kris quickly conceals the spot with her hand, but Red Herring can see a thin stripe of blue between Kris' fingers. Kris yells, "You scratched me, you careless bitch!"

Curiosity overcoming her, Red asks, "Why is your cheek all blue?"

Kris, menacing, daring her to contradict, says, "That's my acne medicine."

Tamara intervenes by changing the subject. "This is a big place. We're gonna have to split up to find a way out."

Kris declares, "That's what *I* was going to say."

The girls start to pair up on their own, but Kris says, "Oh no. *I* decide who goes with who. It's Nada and Tam. I get to keep an eye on Red! And then you guys," indicating the last two.

Munzi says to Patti, "I guess I'm stuck with you."

The designated exploring pairs scatter, some heading up the stairs while others go to see what remains of the lower level.

Nada and Tamara clamor through the house, examining the weird surroundings. Mold spots the walls. The distraction of investigating checks their frantic impulse to escape. They are actually content with their assignment but must grumble on principle.

Nada says, "I don't know why Kris is in charge. She's a bully."

Trying to be companionable and ignore the irony, Tamara says, "That's what a gang is. Anyway, she was first. I joined second, so being second in line is fair."

"You, her second-in-command? You and what weak American army?"

"Cool your Russian MiG jets, Nada," says Tamara, trying a few cupboard doors. "Nothing is set in stone, and if you help get us out of here, you can be our… 'Mistress of War.'"

"Thank you." Says Nada rolling her eyes to the Heavens and throwing up her hands in a that's-the-least-you-can-do gesture.

"This place is sure air-tight. The mold is burning my nostrils."

"You're lucky. I haven't had any sense of smell since I smashed my nose in the ring."

"You told me before." Just then Tamara finds an enormous safe behind the largest of the doors. It's taller than her by half. "Woo, look at this. Jackpot! I'm from a long line of safe crackers." She does a reverse knuckle crack and goes to work on it. Noticing that Nada is not elated, she says, "Oh yeah. Things got pretty messed-up back home, huh?"

"In and out of the wrestling ring… My family sent me here to America to be a superstar and so far I've done nothing. Some promoter said he'd make me a partner, then he took all my money. Us Russians live with scams on a daily basis but somehow I fell for that one."

"You don't have to be defensive. We've all done stuff we're not proud of. I don't even talk to my mom anymore. She gives all her time working for the enemy—the IRS. It's always a management conference, or tax season, or get-ready-for-tax-season—what about Tamara season?"

"What about duck season?" Nada mopes.

"Why don't I get any attention? Well she'll soon see that I'm grown-up and need help when I have my baby. It'll prove she hasn't looked at me in nine months."

"That's just it," says Nada. "I don't even write to my mother. I am so ashamed. I dishonor my family."

"We're your family, Nada. The gang. We're here for you." Flailing at the uncooperative safe, she says, "Why the hell didn't my father teach me anything about how to do this?"

"I am third-in-command then, yes?

Tamara pats her stomach. "Well, my unborn baby is third, but you run a close fourth. Hold up. I just remembered. I've got instructions from dad on me. I've been carrying them for years." She digs a folded paper out of her shoe, rears back at the smell of her foot, and flattens the creases out. She reads aloud, "'Use the shoe you just took off and tap it on the dial. Now wrap your laces around the dial and spin.' These directions are ridiculous. That's not going to help it open."

"Try anyway."

Tamara does the shoe tap and spin, and then Nada joins her effort and together they haul back on the bar to see if it will come loose. It's to no avail. Nada quickly loses interest and shrugs.

"Damn, I guess my father's so-called instructions

were all a joke, another joke on me." Tamara lands a frustrated kick on the safe. Its metal hide doesn't even suffer a scuff mark.

Inside that safe, however, resides Dawn's statue of Kali. And with Tamara's disrespectful kick, the real deity stirs. Kali's avatar is easy to rouse, for it was to this house that her projected consciousness was inexpertly summoned by Dawn.

Searching for a way out, but larcenous nonetheless, Munzi and Patti range around a room that seems to have been the most recently refurbished and least barren, with calming off-white furniture and baby-blue walls. They paw through any abandoned trinkets they can find, which is precious little. Finally they settle on the couch, seizing on a rare chance to talk alone.

"What got you into this stuff?" Munzi asks. "Why isn't a smart girl like you at home with your mom and dad?"

Patti finds one of the few things there are to find, a worthless bangle that she stuffs into her pocket. "I got busted for shoplifting. I can't help myself."

Munzi says, "So Pattycakes is a shoplifter? Wait, that's your whole gig?"

Patti says defensively, "People do a lot of community service for shoplifting. I used to stuff it all over me. Inside too."

Munzi says, "I want a real secret out of you. You must have done something more heinous before you joined us."

"Sure. I made out with..." Patti seems to regret her revelation before it escapes her treacherous mouth.

"Who?"

"I shouldn't..."

"Who?" Munzi cries. "I'm dying here."

"Father Patrick." There it is. Patti has a bombshell after all.

"The Father? Forget shoplifting. You're going to hell for sure."

"Do you know him?"

"He came on to me, too. I told him I wanted to be a nun. He told me I shouldn't let my 'sweet ass' go to waste."

Patti bursts out laughing even before Munzi can finish.

"What?" Munzi demands.

Still laughing, Patti says, "Wait, so you would have been *Nun*zi?"

In a righteous huff, Munzi says, "Hey, I could still be a nun. It could happen."

This sends Patti into new paroxysms of laughter. "What, you want to redeem yourself like a five-cent deposit bottle?"

"Ha ha! Maybe we should just keep our shit to ourselves. Just shut up and let me think how we're going to get out of here."

"All right, I have another secret. But I'll pipe down."

Ever a sucker for dirt, Munzi yelps, "No, you can't leave it hanging out like that." Then she switches tactics. Whipping off her jacket and using it to fashion a faux nun's wimple, she says, "You need to tell the good Sister your confession."

It's on. Knocking a bunch of knickknacks onto the floor, including a mysterious cloaked object, Munzi and Patti put two chairs together to form a makeshift confession booth.

Having established the right atmosphere, Munzi continues, "Let me hear all the dirtiest, grossest stuff you've done, my child, and I will tell you how many Hail Marys you need to set you free of your sins."

Triumphantly, Patti says, "I didn't just make out with Father Patrick. I fucked him in the back room of the church. Late, after hours."

Accidentally brushing her hand against the shrouded object which tingles with a sparkling flash of energy, Munzi is suddenly, unwillingly, and unwittingly aroused. She gasps, "This is heavy stuff. What did he… kiss like?"

"You're a nun," Patti teases. "You really want to know?"

Under a mystic influence that acts on her like an inhibition remedy, Munzi breathes, "Yes. Try it out on me."

"What do you mean?

Dispensing with foreplay, Munzi seizes the nerd gang member for a long hard kiss. Patti succumbs to her advances. In her flailing, newly-tested, clumsy girl-on-girl lovemaking, Munzi knocks the covering off the mysterious object, a large, ornate and ancient phallus. It lands on the floor like a pornographic spinner pointing back at her and she scoops it up.

"Whoa. Look at that crazy old fuck stick," Munzi croons with admiration. The object glows from a single large jewel, bringing in erotic Indian *thumri* music that only

Munzi can hear. Sitar cords ride atop rhythmic drumming that swells slowly, an ecstatic woman's voice soars wordlessly. Munzi is aware that a spirit has taken full control of her. She doesn't care. For the moment, she prefers its company to her own angst and avarice. Bathed in the influence, she says with wonder, "It's like Cleopatra's dildo or something."

Then Patti takes hold of it. "No, it's not Egyptian."

The icon glows in Patti's hands too. She hears the music now too, affected in a similar way, not quite herself anymore, but still nerd enough to continue the analysis. She blows off the dust and paws at the base. "It's ancient Indian. There's an inscription. But I can't read it."

Munzi says, "Let's figure it out together, smart girl. We can use this thing. Trust me."

They embrace again. Munzi starts peppering kisses on Patti's neck. Patti surprises herself by putting up no resistance. In a moment, she has to admit to herself that she is into it full-tilt.

They start to undress, taking their tops off and pressing together in bliss.

Soon Patti is in full submission, sprawled out on the couch, glasses tossed away who-knows-where. Munzi straddles atop her and notices for the first time just how pretty Patti's face is – smooth skin, long lashes, wavy ash-blond hair swirling wildly. Munzi's attention is soon brought to Patti's long, lavender-scented throat, then her ample bosom, straining against a lacy, strapless, yellow brassiere. Her tongue is making the whole tour from there and back to Patti's hungry mouth. One of her hands drops to Patti's crotch. Then the spirit allows Munzi one clear thought: *Run over and shut the door!* She whips around.

Too late.

Tamara, Nada, Kris and Red Herring stand there together in the doorway, startling them. Munzi draws a breath to launch into a this-isn't-what-it-looks-like denial, but she can see in their crude expressions that it would be a useless exercise.

Instead, Munzi asks, "How long have you gawkers been standing there?"

Tamara, who had entered first, says, "Long enough."

Nada, elbowing her way to the front, says, "What are you doing, Munzi? You hate that bisexual stuff." She snatches the phallus away from them and gets her own dose of otherworldly energy. The flash that emanates from the jewel takes the form of visible light yet none of them can register it consciously.

Quickly getting dressed, Munzi says, "I'm not sure what happened. It was innocent."

Indian music rises in Nada's head and takes her over. Looking at Patti hungrily, Nada says, "Maybe it was up till now. I'm kind of into watching her get it though." Easily corrupted to a complete reprobate by a small dose of magic, Nada lets Munzi swipe the phallus back. In the process it barely glances against Kris, who is even more easily corrupted.

The outnumbered Patti begins to sober. "You know what? I'm not into it anymore. Maybe we should put that thing away."

Nada snorts, "You're not into it, huh? Maybe you have no choice in the matter."

Nada grabs Patti in the throat-framing hold that wrestler's call a Full Nelson while Kris flips up Patti's mid-length denim skirt with a flourish.

Firmly in command of the phallus again, Munzi offers, "You want me to stick it in, Patti?

"No."

"Are you sure?" asks Munzi. "You'll make Cleopatra angry."

Dreamily, Nada says, "I like the name Cleopatra."

Kris pulls down Patti's panties and runs her fingers through the bush, which is still wet from before.

Patti cries, "Stop!" She tries to shake her head emphatically but has little leeway.

Munzi says, "Looks like there's working batteries in this big old glow toy."

Red Herring protests, "It's too big. Don't do it!"

Munzi brandishes the phallus at Red. "You want to be next, pigeon?"

Patti yells, "Stop! You're gonna do a Fatty Arbuckle on me." The others look confused. Nobody gets the reference. "He killed a girl by sticking a bottle in her in 1921."

"Tamara says, "1921? Girl, if anyone ever knew what you were talking about, you'd be in a lot of trouble." To Munzi, she adds, I want to see this bitch get it for all her wising off to us lately."

Kris asserts her leadership saying, in her best mocking voice, "Yeah, get her. She loves it. Big know-it-all, never-been-kissed is losing her virginity at the prom."

"No-o-o!" Patti cries.

Munzi points the phallus at Patti. "Would that turn you on, you lezzie weasel? I know it would work for me."

Patti's struggles in vain, but before Munzi can do anything, they hear the opening bars of Munzi's ring tone,

"Pop Goes The Weasel."

Kris attributes it to Patti. "You've got a musical cunt?"

Digging out her phone, Munzi says, "Hold up you guys. Quiet."

Nada clamps Patti's mouth while she struggles.

In her sweetest voice, Munzi croons, "Hi mom! ... No, I'm great ... I'm with the girls ...you liked my present? I know, that shade of pink is so hard to get ... I'm glad ... love to Dad ... yeah, stayin' out of trouble, love you too."

Munzi holds out the telephone so that others can hear more clearly.

In a sticky apple pie voice reminiscent of the days of the Impala that they drove in with, her mom says, "Tell everyone I said to have fun, sweetie."

Patti tries to respond, only to exclaim, "Mmmph!"

Munzi says to her mom brightly, "I will."

She hangs up and nestles her cell phone back in her jeans pocket. "Aww, she said to have fun." Switching just as easily to a psycho gear, she announces, "Patti doesn't look like she's having *enough* fun."

"Nada says, "I can fix that. Nothing like a little autoerotic asphyxiation to make the orgasm a big one."

Choking out the words, still trying to be the intellectual at all costs, Patti croaks, "It's not *auto*erotic if you're doing it to me."

"Wise mouth." Nada redoubles her efforts to shut Patti up as Red Herring warns, "She can't breathe."

Gang banger or not, Kris has to draw the line somewhere. She says, "All right, joke's over."

Even Tamara says, "This is too far."

The other girls, except for Munzi who is hypnotized by the phallus, struggle with Nada to try to stop her, but the wrestler is too strong. Kris, who is closest, gets shoved back with Nada's hand in her face, taking another scratch to the bargain.

Alarmed beyond reason, their leader runs from the room shouting, "My face!"

Patti thrashes around and then drops to the floor like a discarded rag doll.

As the magic drains from the last combatants, Munzi pulls back and her eyes widen in horror at what they did.

Red Herring chokes on her own tears.

"She's dead!" Red wails. "You guys are in big trouble! You killed her!"

Chapter 12
Kali Invoked

Interlude: What Has Gone Unsaid

Very few can recall what happened to Dawn. It was between her and the demons. Witchcraft was her vice. Her husband Burl forbid its practice.

Right after they married, Dawn got pregnant and all the work of renovating the new bed and breakfast fell to Burl.

What's more, Burl wouldn't have sex with Dawn while she was pregnant, but the horniness made her crazy. Since Burl was too busy to keep an eye on her, she found herself taking secret trips to the woods "to be by herself." She visited a man down on the other side of the stream named, Damon Heckler, who satisfied her cravings.

After one such trip, only halfway home, Dawn felt a popping sensation and the flood commenced. She collapsed on a wooden stump, her gaudy '80's dress soaking up fluids that gushed like a fire hose.

"Burl!" she called out. "Damon!" she yelled. "My water broke!" No one heard or no one wanted to come.

In an old habit that had served her well in years past, she closed her eyes, visualizing midnight blue skin hung with severed heads and arms. Thick, cloying music filled her head.

"Kali, I summon you, get me through this! I beg of you! Kaaaaliiii!"

She saw no manifestation of Kali's form, but she noticed that the trees where she had stopped, great boughs bent like worshippers, formed a kind of alter over her. They trembled and bent even further as a cold wind rose. Just when she expected to push, the baby's head emerged as though it were pulled from her. In the next moment, the entire baby came flying out with such force that it snapped the umbilical cord.

Somehow she had delivered a healthy baby "by herself" and everything seemed fine. They called the baby girl Kristine.

Burl knew that Dawn had given birth in the woods, suspected dark arts, and warned, "Your bad reputation is driving our business to hell."

"Yes," she agreed, "but we can squelch those rumors. Now that I'm a mother it's time I put the whole Kali thing behind me." Maybe she believed what she said. After all, she hadn't actually seen Kali appear. The birth seemed unusual but in all her years it was her first, and what did she know?

The rumors about her being a witch eventually faded. Still, few wanted to spend the night at Bonnie's B&B. The damage was done.

By the time Gary the magician came to town, years later, Burl no longer openly admitted he had anything to do with the ownership of Bonnie's B&B. Burl found work as a handyman and employed Gary to do odd jobs.

As Bonnie's fell into disrepair, Gary knocked a few nails in, among other things. The hotel was an albatross, and Gary's great virtue was that he was discreet. He heard the screams from the house when Burl took out his frustrations on his wife.

For his part, Burl had the stubborn notion that Dawn was still practicing witchcraft, even though her supernatural paraphernalia was collecting dust in the garage. The gear was there for a reason though. Dawn worried that when her daughter reached puberty, she would have to deal with the spirit of Kali demanding repayment, so she held fast to the weapons of black mass destruction.

When Kristine turned thirteen, Gary moved into that garage and turned it into a make-shift apartment.

For every year that the young girl aged, Dawn seemed to age eight years. Burl was too drunk most of the time to look at his wife's face when he was not punching it. He thought the wrinkles were scars from the beatings. Given her circumstances, putting aside the tools of witchcraft for a decade or two was not enough. Dawn believed in Evil, invested in it the way Sardar would later invest in the products of Wall Street. When she gave birth, Evil invested in her. She was a long-term asset by witch standards; the blink of an eye by Kali's. And besides, Dawn and Evil needed each other more than ever.

Chapter 13
Ancient Totems

Dawn reposes in the big stuffed chair in Sardar's living room, still wearing nothing but her black panties, a bra, and his raspberry-orange robe. She gazes up at him as he buttons his blue-checked, hand-stitched, Egyptian cotton shirt. Although a large brass statue of Kali brandishing her weapons and standing on a dead man dominates the table, it is the large phallic totem next to Kali that catches Dawn's eye. Seeing the room for the first time with daylight streaming in, she notices that Sardar owns a whole collection of smaller sexual totems. Apparently creeped out, she asks, "What are those things?"

"Just some items I've picked up over the years."

"Ancient totems," she pouts. "Why was it all penises and vaginas with the ancient Hindus?"

"They're supposed to keep the evil eye and bad luck at bay. To me, they're just art."

Dawn calls out in pain and covers her neck in shocked surprise, an outraged expression darkening her features.

"Oh they're not that bad, Dawn."

Dawn wails in anguish.

"You're serious? What's the problem?"

With growing discomfort, Dawn says, "There's something happening. I have a vision. My daughter and some girls she's with. They're in trouble!"

"You know where they are?"

"No, I can't ..." she manages to force out before

being compelled to scream, then finishes her thought with her next breath, "… tell that much. Ohhh."

"What's happening?"

Invisible spirits hurl Dawn to the ground. She holds her neck, struggling against the unseen force and trying to scream.

"Help! They're holding me down. It hurts. I can't breathe!"

Sardar, seeing nothing, tries to help but doesn't know how. He says, "I'll get you a glass of water," and rushes out of the room.

While he is gone, she battles her way back to the comfort of the stuffed chair before being stricken anew. For a moment, she is completely immobile. Overcome by spasms – death throes? – her elbows and knees all straighten out and lock. She is a windmill stuck still by terror. Then she slumps back into the chair, panting and exhausted.

Sardar reenters with the useless glass of water. Dawn's neck is mottled by strangulation marks so thorough they could almost be rope burn.

"You wanted proof, Sardar? That thing almost killed me. I could see the face of evil coming down at me. I could see the house. The old bed and breakfast."

"Take this." Sardar hands over the water.

She drinks, if only to not offend the man to whom she is a supplicant. "Sardar, what's happening to me?"

Cornered, Sardar says, "Okay! They're not just art! But some events are beyond explanation and shouldn't be too closely examined."

"Sardar, if you know something about this, anything

at all, don't hold out on me. I don't know anything!"

Sardar takes a knee and clasps her hand like a man proposing. "I can tell you what I think we may be dealing with. Only the adepts in the cult of Shiva-Dionysus who practice the bacchanalia can save the world from destruction. They're trying to do that in their own way."

"Save the world from who?"

"Kali. The Trampler. The most powerful of all deities. Something has disturbed her."

Her chin held high to brandish the gory proof, Dawn says, "You believe me now, don't you?"

Chapter 14
I'm Gonna Yank on This One

Munzi, Tamara and Red Herring, not exactly an avenging posse of the virtuous, gather around Nada for whatever lame explanation she cares to provide.

Nada says, "That wasn't me back there."

Munzi quickly adds, "It wasn't me either. It was like some strange force was making me act that way. I'm not a bad person. I don't do stuff like that."

"Poor Patti," sighs Nada. "She died in my arms. But like a boa constrictor I kept squeezing. It was like someone else was in my head telling me to kill. I had no choice."

Tamara sizes it up. "We are royally fucked. We're going to death row for this."

On that note, Munzi says, "Nobody else saw anything. Nobody else knows."

Tamara's head snaps up in alarm. "Where's Kris? She's always warning us about squealing, and she's the one that's probably calling the cops now."

Munzi says, "Kris is not gonna call the police. We're *wanted* by the police. Anyway, it was an honest mistake, Patti's death. An accident, right girls?"

Red Herring sobs, "I can't say that. I won't say that."

Tamara grabs her. "That's exactly what you'll say. I am not having my baby in jail."

"Well," says Red Herring, "we can't just leave Patti like that. I'm going back in there."

Kris has been gone for quite some time at this point.

Tamara never really played up her second-in-command role. Munzi and Nada both wanted it more and, to keep the peace, she has never before asserted any sort of authority. Not her style. Tamara's only distinction, in her own mind, is that she has known Kris the longest by a couple weeks. But now even her rivals are looking at her.

Tamara says, "What do you want to do, Red, bury her in the damn living room? We can't get out of here."

Nada, still fueled by self-pity, says, "I am not even a citizen. They will deport me for sure and then I will hang. Nothing left. Nada."

Tamara says, "First we need to find Kris. If she's on her cell phone talking to the cops, we have to kill her, too."

"We are not killers," Munzi insists.

Kris decompresses in the bathroom, finding more and more blue invading her face. "Damn, this is getting crazy."

She runs water and takes her shirt off, finding and swiping at blue patches blooming all over her body.

"I wish none of this ever happened," she mutters to herself. "If we didn't jump the girl, if we didn't take the car, if we didn't show up here, then Patti wouldn't be dead."

Kris begins to apply make-up on her shoulder, finds another spot and more. She throws down the brush, frustrated. There's just too much area to cover.

"This isn't working. I have to start all over on this stupid make-up."

Nada pounds on the table in a perfect dovetail for the unseen Kris' frustration.

Tamara says, "Let's get our stories straight."

"Ok," says Nada. "It's not my fault." Staring daggers at Red Herring now, she says, "Nobody had better say it's my fault."

"Nobody will," Tamara assures her.

Unconvinced, Nada counters, "How about I murder you all? Nobody else knows me here in America."

Red says, "Why are we turning against each other instead of working on getting out?"

Tamara says, "Nada, don't sweat it. You have nothing to worry about."

Red Herring cries, "Why are you telling Nada don't sweat it? It's, like, totally her fault and nobody else's."

Tamara says, "Because Nada and her strength is what's gonna get us out of here. Isn't it Nada?"

Nada says, "What do you have in mind?"

Tamara warms up to her new idea. "We checked out the windows on this level. They're sealed up tight. But there has to be a lot more openings in a house this big, and maybe they're not that secure."

The four of them together – no more splitting up! – move along as the cohesive unit they always wished they could be, exploring the decrepit main building. They stick their heads into room after room, following the south wall, the tantalizing daylight. The windows bring only a promising glow however. There is no breeze through the cracks, no fresh air to remind them what it is like to take a breath without tasting must. The bedrooms are all dusty with occasional wisps of rodent turd but are otherwise what one would expect of a typical B&B just waiting for a fresh coat of paint before reopening for the season. Nothing on the walls more jarring than oil paintings of ships on rough seas. Nothing on the shelving more distressing than chipped Delft porcelain.

But there are some special rooms that make it seem that the building is accustomed to supplying more than just bed and breakfast. In that vein, Red Herring, Munzi, Nada and Tamara come upon a workroom. What kind of work went on there, though, is open to speculation. Considering the ornate array of bronze idols, shrines, and the framed art depicting death, brutality and painfully deviant sex, nothing can be ruled out. The four pick their way through carefully because whatever once went on in there, it was done with so much abandon that eldritch objects are scattered all over the bare-concrete floor.

"Why are there so many crazy places in here?" Tamara complains.

Munzi says, "I don't know. Makes me want to keep moving."

Red stops them. "Look at this. She points to an ornate window-like wooden frame against the wall with ancient symbols on it. Considering the row of blackened, drippy candles on its shelf the arrangement looks very much like an altar. Through the arch they can see a single panel painted black.

Munzi says, "A boarded up window on top of the force field? That's gonna be even harder to get through. You're killing me, Red."

"Wait," Red Herring calls to their retreating backs, "this one is different. I can touch it."

Nada gives it a hands-on examination with growing excitement. "I can feel a cool wind blowing through. I think it's outside air."

"I can too," says Tamara. "It could be a way out."

Nada flushes away the candles in one brute swipe, slips her fingers under a handhold in the black panel and tries to lift it like any other window. She fails. "Must be stuck like that for years. Stand back. I'm gonna yank on this one."

Nada gets a better grip and braces herself. After two hard pulls that gain nothing, she replants her feet, and calls upon a monumental effort. With tendons straining in her neck, and fingernails splintering, one last grunt raises and wedges the panel just to the width of an athletic young woman. "That's as much as it goes. It's wide enough though."

Bending slightly, they see the foliage of the grounds outside and they cheer. The crisp scent of autumn leaves wafts in – a smell of decay, certainly, but a good decay, one that promises rest before renewal.

Red jumps up and down. "You did it."

Tamara, Munzi and Red Herring rush to the opening. Nada pushes them out of the way. "Hey, I'm first-in-command now. Americans go second."

Tamara says, "Okay, it's your thing. I get it. Lead the way."

Nada leans across the mysterious carvings.

Her body is in the mousetrap, but she luxuriates, looking down at the view from the second floor.

Tamara says, "What do you see out there?"

Nada hangs out the window exulting at the fresh air and daylight. "This is it," she cries. "Freedom!"

An inscription on the carvings softly glows just as she raises her hands and eyes up to Heaven. With a fairy dust wish-granting twinkle, the casement she has jammed in place comes free. The thin panel rapidly slides down to slice her like a midsection guillotine, making a sickening squelch. She doesn't even have time to scream.

Blood pours out of her pants leg. The girls gasp.

In the stunned silence, Nada's lower body remains stuck in place.

The girls cannot believe it. Maybe it's like a magician's cutaway, the rounded slide where no one gets hurt! That's why she didn't scream. In a minute she's going to laugh at how stupid they all are. Only they don't really *think* that so much as *wish* that. They approach slowly and silently as though they were sneaking up on Death itself, and it might not catch them if they held their breath.

Tamara touches the seat of Nada's jeans gently like she's trying to wake her up, and the half-body drops away, intestines flying from the cut section, liberated blood spraying. They are all horrified, screaming, out of their minds scared.

Red Herring is the most familiar with this sense of panic. While she continues to shriek and tremble uncontrollably, there is a quiet corner of her mind that observes the other two behaving exactly the same way: *Tamara and Munzi are just as frightened as I am.* When the strong girls go down that's a helluva lot scarier. Even worse is what happens next.

Tamara, intrepid explorer that she is, shakes off her fright and touches the panel the way she tested the skull in the basement. She's not ready to make a joke out of it. After all, this shit is real, but she's got the cat-killing curiosity-pull. From that gentle contact off the hot magic comes another starburst twinkle and her quick mind seems to fill with the music of the destroyer god, the sort of blood-lust beat that must have accompanied the ancient purges of good and evil. Her eyes dance down to the severed lower half of Nada and her lips skin back in a feral smile. She crouches and her fingers dip like a ladle into cooking sauce. She has the blood on her tongue and decides that the meal is ready. She snatches the loose end of a mile of intestine, gets it deep in her teeth and tears into the spongy sheath the same way she attacks a good calamari.

Like a contact high, the sick urge leaks to Red and then to Munzi, who is even closer. Munzi leans toward the carcass as Tamara chews, and Red's screams rise to a whole new level.

Chapter 15
Crawl

Another leisurely day as Dawn putters around Sardar's kitchen, playing house. "Do you have another can opener, Gary? This one is full of old gunk."

"Yes," he brightens. They've once again enjoyed each other's company as nature's own remedy for what the harrowing search has put them through. Sardar is actually whistling as he pulls a new can opener from a bag and cuts it free of its plastic bubble and cardboard. Then he frowns and says, "Crap."

"What's wrong?"

"I thought I needed one of these when I bought the damn thing, and after opening it I just realized that I already had a spare one in the cupboard."

"Are you very badly upset?" she asks with a smile. "Is there something I can kiss to make it all better?"

Back to his amorous haze, Sardar suggests, "I have a book with a lot of good positions."

Dawn's eyes light up with something other than lust. "Oh shit, my daughter. We'd better go."

"Right. Your daughter and the rest of them. What were we thinking?"

They dress hastily in whatever clothes they've strewn around. Dawn can hear the girls' excited shouts echoing softly through her head as she and Sardar are on their way out the door. Dawn, now dressed in a blue, low-cut sheath, grabs her waist and spits up breakfast and blood.

"What's happening?" Sardar implores.

Struggling to recover, Dawn manages to gasp out, "One of the girls…she was … cut in half."

The psychic attack weakens her knees, but again falls short of killing her.

Scarcely knowing whether to believe it, Sardar asks, "Cut? In half? You can see that? What girls are these? More visions?"

"It's not just visions. I feel it too. Eww, they're eating the guts now and that's making me taste it with them. Ohh, it's disgusting."

Sardar shakes his head. "This search is killing you. We can't go on."

"Don't worry about me," she says with a rattling cough. "We have to get to them. Save them."

Munzi is the first to collect herself. She enters the master bathroom to splash some water on her face and wash her abused taste buds just as Kris is finishing her make-up. The room is clouded to its vaulted ceilings like a steam bath from the open tap of hot water flowing into the sink.

"So this is where you are, Kris? You don't give a damn about what's happening to us in this house, do you?"

"What are you talking about? I've got this whole situation under control."

"We murdered Patti back there. And Nada's dead, too. Don't you have any conscience?"

"Wait, Nada?" Kris sounds surprised but not entirely upset. She doesn't make eye contact with Munzi. Rather, she keeps staring at herself in the mirror, obsessed with a transformation that goes far beyond that from life to death.

"She got sliced by a window while you were kissing a powder puff."

"Are you questioning me? Are you challenging my leadership?

"Yes."

"Well I have a plan. As always."

"Well so far your plans have sucked for us, and two people are dead because of it."

"I didn't coop us up in here. I didn't even want to come here. You ladies got stir crazy and got horny. So what? And Nada probably killed herself out of guilt. Chalk up one less terrorist for the U.S. of A."

"I knew you didn't give a shit."

Kris continues with her make-up. "No one ever looks out for me so I say 'fuck 'em'."

"Is that right?"

"One second." Kris pulls her cell phone out of its charger. She slides it open to make a call.

Munzi says, "So the girls were right. You are calling the cops on us."

Munzi lunges at Kris, grabbing the phone out of her hand. Kris's immediate response – wheeling around to deliver a stinging open-hand slap to her face, forces Munzi to rock on her heels.

Bouncing back with her tough girl best, the Munz plants a fist in Kris's solar plexus, and that blow should have been pivotal. But the fight cannot last long as Munzi's punch is stunningly ineffective. Kris, suddenly possessed of unnatural strength and constitution, barely feels the blow. She grips Munzi by, of all things, the jaw, like she is a beast, fighting another beast. Munzi should be able to slide easily out of what looks like a pinch to the face, but something is sapping her. Struggle though she might, she is ultimately led wherever Kris directs her. With her other hand, Kris turns up the faucet in the sink so that scalding hot water floods the basin.

Kris dunks and holds a helpless Munzi under the churning heat as the room continues to steam up to a complete white out. Sensing that she might still have need for her victim – at least until her transformation is complete – Kris relents without even a comment.

Rubbing her sore jaw, but in no position to retaliate, Munzi spots the broken phone, and despite herself, gets angry all over again. "Who ... the fuck ... were you calling?"

"I just wanted someone to get us out of here."

"No cops," Munzi reminds her. Meanwhile one of them has bumped into a switch. They hear the generator hum joined by a metallic thump. The rising steam begins to clear and Munzi's gaze follows it upward as it vanishes into a newly opened vent. "Wait a minute. A vent! There's gotta be a bigger vent or a crawlspace in a house like this. That's our way out."

Munzi turns up bruised and battered as she and Kris rejoin the other two survivors. Munzi's face is a roadmap of lacerations, her right cheek a four-lane highway dividing around a black-and-blue hill.

Tamara, curious that Munzi is looking worse than ever while seemingly content, asks, "What happened? You look like a train-wreck."

Munzi smiles. "We're getting the hell out of here."

"You have an idea?"

"Yeah. There has to be another way out. A pipe or a vent or a crawl space somewhere high up. I don't even care if it comes out on the roof or whatever. We'll find one of those."

Kris turns to her second in command. "Tamara, you can crawl in between floors and open the outside door."

"Guess what?" says Tamara. "Wrong. Not me. As you already know—and everyone knows because of you—I'm carrying a baby."

Kris says, "Well, I ain't gonna send Red Herring. She's too stupid and has no sense of direction."

Red Herring retorts, "Next year I'll be able to drive a car."

"It's never you taking the risk," says Tamara, "is it, Fearless Leader?"

Kris looks to Munzi. "Well who suggested it?"

Munzi cringes. "Oh, fuck no. I'm not doing it. I hate *elevators*. That closed-in feeling? No way."

With a renewed sense of purpose – mostly – the girls head for the upper levels. Churning through an increasingly uncomfortable and claustrophobic series of rooms and passages, they no longer ask who builds a house like this but are rather grateful that more options exist. In that fragile state, they dare not speak at all. It's only when they get to the very last staircase opening on a space with diagonal roof beams that they feel the grip of their limitations.

"This is our last chance," says Munzi as if she is trying to remind herself. "The attic."

"I don't do attics," says Tamara, coughing away at the stalest air yet.

Red adds an audible but incoherent grumble.

"Get up there," says Kris, prodding her and the others up the last spindly steps.

To find anything that looks at all promising, they have to double back past the open floor with no railing, pass through a narrow throat that has only a shoelace pull-chain to operate a bare bulb, and arrive at a half brick zone with a hatch-like opening in one wall. It gapes, beckoning them with a flooring inside it that slants upward.

Kris points to the wood frame for the hesitating Munzi who has her big flashlight fired up and is pointing it down the continuing hallway. "Get in the hole," says the Garter Snake's leader.

Munzi says, "I told you, no way."

Kris says, "Well there is no way in hell I'm getting in there. I'm the godmother of Tamara's baby." Tamara doesn't bother contradicting her.

Munzi looks to Red Herring, who contributes only a helpless shrug.

Munzi, calling on her Brooklyn courage, pronounces them, "Freakin' idiots," and leans into the hole with her knee on the brink, illuminating the mysterious interior with the light. The shaft is lined with dust and debris, and takes a turn that blocks her view. With one last, "I don't know guys," she climbs up into the crawlspace with her flashlight, finding it difficult and creaky from the outset. Then she makes the turn sideward and upward and parts from her friends, telling herself that the whole ordeal is nearly over. The voices of the others checking on her progress already come to her muted and echoed.

The flashlight she uses gives her some slight comfort in the enclosed space, but causes its own problems. It is one of those wet-cell flood lamps, enough to illumine an entire campsite. Once enclosed with her, it is a glare generator, turning every bolt in every brace into a miniature sun. It is also heavy and clunky in her hands. Munzi remembers how she got it, going through the Impala's glove box after the carjacking, tossing it for anything of worth. There was a tiny, LED light that came attached to an elastic headband. That would have been perfect. But at the time, who could foresee its value?

Munzi can still hear Red Herring's chipper-kid voice, "You see anything? A light ahead?"

"No," says Munzi. "It's getting darker."

Sure enough, the oversized light slowly dims. Who knows when the battery was last recharged? Through the flickering, Munzi sees nothing but warped two-by-four studs and piles of insulation kicking up who-knows-what toxins. She coughs on the flying dust. The beams creak ominously whether she moves or not.

The conversation goes back and forth with Red Herring until Munzi and Red can't hear each other anymore.

Munzi calls out, "Hullo?" Thin as she is, there is no way for her to cope with how the beams converge with distance, and the space narrows until... "I'm stuck. Is anyone listening?"

She tries to free herself, cracking plaster. The light flickers, wavers, and goes dark.

Anxiety turns to terror. Shallow breath becomes no breath. Rapid heartbeat becomes palpitations. The smell of her own sweat combines with that of her urine.

"Shit!"

A desperate bang on the battery gets the flashlight going again as Munzi continues to squeeze herself out. She is no longer committed to going forward, but the two-by-fours won't let her go back. Some spirit in the wood seems to revel in the song of creaking and crackling that follows Munzi's lithe figure. The song builds into a crescendo. An important beam goes *snap*!

Munzi, realizing her fate, says one last, "fuck!" An ill wind blows out her flashlight like a mere candle, and the crawlspace collapses on her in a rumbling crescendo.

The girls hear the sound of destruction. Plaster and dust blow back out of the opening Munzi disappeared into. The clatter and boom is like a mine collapse, the presumed cave-in shattering their faith, eliciting startled screams of "Oh my God, no!"

In the new silence the last thing they hear is Munzi's cell phone ring tone playing her out with one final sound bite of "Pop Goes the Weasel," a lively *Bup-a-bup, a-buh buh buh bum...*

Chapter 16
Up the River

Interlude: What Has Gone Unsaid

In 1988, daughter Kris and husband Burl both disappeared. Dawn naturally asked the local police to investigate her loss. What Salem authorities came up with was a theory that the rumored witch had murdered them both, burying their bodies somewhere on the extensive property. They searched Bonnie's top to bottom, scrubbed the grounds for clues, and found blood evidence but no bodies. She was promptly arrested on suspicion.

By spell or negligence, they somehow forgot to check the small murky pool, which would have made a terrible hiding place anyway. They were sure that any bodies would have been in the extensive and impossible-to-search swampland nearby.

"I didn't kill my daughter!" She pleaded.

"Then who did?" an officer replied coldly.

"Find Burl, that son-of-a-bitch! He did it and went on the run! I'm not lying!"

He looked at her face to see if he could detect any trace of falsehood. He was shocked to see that Dawn had the porcelain skin of a teenager, and that skin did not so much as twitch. She was just too good, too calm in the midst of all that tragic loss. He said, "How could you do it?"

Smiling sweetly, she asked, "You wouldn't send me to jail, would you?"

"I hope they send you to Hell," the Sheriff replied.

"Where else?" Dawn said under her breath.

They hauled her away as startled young Gary looked on.

The trial played out like a classic Salem witch hunt. The judge cared very little for evidence and she went straight to the pen, a big surprise for her.

In prison, Dawn's wrinkles blossomed again during her lengthy sentence. Trapped and aging, she went stir crazy, and on one particularly batty day, when she sensed that she had a use for it, sliced out the plump tongue of her pretty cell mate.

Chapter 17
Score!

Dawn and Sardar arrive at the old mansion, hopeful that they can make a difference there. They actually sneak up on the place, going through the forested path through a rear gate in case the danger is immediate. Sardar shrugs uncomfortably from the bulky holstered Taser under his jacket. He reaches for it, but changes his mind. He can't wave it around just because he doesn't like wearing it. It's probably useless anyway.

Dawn speaks softly. "This is the place I saw in the vision. I think some of the girls are still alive. I feel that someone is."

Sardar squints through the trees. From where he stands, the back of the house looks serene. "Bonnie's B&B? Are you sure we're in the right place?"

"They're here somewhere. I'm just not sure what part of the house they're in. They may have separated."

"Well we're not going to split up. We are dealing with Kali, Goddess of Transcendental Night, Cosmic Dancer, a Trampler, and Devourer of the dead. I'm not leaving you."

Seeing Dawn's odd reaction to his description of Kali, Sardar looks away.

Six girls walked into the house only a few hours earlier. Now only three are alive and accounted for: Kris, Tamara and Red Herring. They drained the life out of

Patti. They saw Nada chopped in half. As for Munzi, there is no way of telling if she is dead yet. She is not answering as they call out to her, but that does not mean the forces in the house have dispatched her as they disposed of her friends. Tamara holds out hope that she may just be unconscious or living through some unimaginable torture. Red fantasizes that Munzi has escaped and is already out of earshot, soon to be returning with another stolen car to whisk them all out of harm's way.

Kris seems pretty sure Munzi is dead, though. It is disconcerting how sure she is, so smug in her every move. Even more disconcerting, though, is how cheery she is, how more-than-OK with it she is.

"If there's any chance Munzi is still alive," says Tamara, "we have to help her."

"Yes," says Red, appealing to Kris, "please."

Kris shrugs in answer. "Yeah, why not?"

They follow the attic space approximately under the passage Munzi took, Kris gamely leading the way. Although the walls are otherwise bare, a space near the end of the hall features an antique carved stick mounted on a decorative plaque. From a tapered barb pointed to the ground, it widens out to a handle and base distinguished by a large, brightly painted eye with a heavy blue lid and black lashes. The eye slowly blinks before they even notice it hanging there. Yes, it is painted. Yes, it blinks.

Grabbing it off its base and giving it a twirl, the gang leader sings out, "Score!" Then she searches the ceiling with it like a water-seeking diviner. "By now, Munzi would be somewhere up in here," she says with a poke topside.

The more-than-a-hint of mockery in Kris's demeanor

suggests she is merely playing along. Kris jabs her new toy at the ceiling tiles, narrow end first. "I wish I could tear a hole with this, but it's not sharp enough."

Tamara says, "Forget that. There's a ladder right here, you idiot." Her patience with Kris is about at an end. Leader and follower no longer define them.

As Kris and Red join her, Tamara begins to climb the ladder, saying, "Hold it steady, please."

Kris says, "Careful. You're pregnant."

Tamara stops and turns. "Thanks again for reminding me," she says. "Unless your job is pointing out the obvious, you haven't been a lot of help around here."

Kris gives an elaborate and innocent shrug as if she cannot imagine what Tamara means. *"Moi?"*

Continuing up the few rungs to the low ceiling, Tamara manages to wrestle the hatch aside in a shower of dirt that leaves Red Herring coughing below her. The opening reveals a tall, dizzying turbine shaft into which she shouts "Munzi!! Munz?"

No answer, and she's afraid to climb up any further until the hatch is entirely out of the way but she can't push it anymore.

Groping the air below her and not connecting with anything, Tamara demands, "Gimme that stick."

Kris extends it but pulls it back playfully when it is almost in Tamara's hand.

"C'mon, Kris, what's wrong with you? Give that to me."

Kris extends the rod again, holding the offering steady, but a tad short this time.

Overextending herself, Tamara teeters and falls off the ladder in Kris' direction. The two tumble down, the stick penetrating Tamara's back with a *ka-chunk*.

Red is too focused on the ladder and what might be on top of it to realize the disaster that unfolded. When she looks back, Kris is sitting on the floor still holding the eyestick by the handle, trying to peek around for a better look. Tamara sits nestled in front of her with the stick disappearing under her shirt in back. On the other side of her, it reappears in a genuine through-and-through staking, her tiny fetus stuck way out on the pointy end, trailing its umbilical cord. It is pink, about four inches long, half of that is head, the other half wrapped around the stick. It was perfectly healthy seconds ago, and ebbing into death now. It has no voice with which to scream, but the girls are horrified by a squishing sound as life saps away. Red Herring stands frozen in disbelief, *But she wasn't high enough for that! The damned thing wasn't pointy enough to do that! And Kris looks more curious than unhappy.*

As the blood drools out of Tamara's mouth, it makes a squishy sound until the last of it goes drip, drip, drip, and Red screams her famous scream.

Outside, the house has made it clear that it wants no more intruders. It deigned to let the Garter Snakes in because it had a purpose for them – for one of them at least. But it will not open its doors to Sardar and Dawn.

First they try brute strength, of course. Then tools. Then Sardar supplicates the house, implores it, threatens it. All else failing, Sardar begs the intercession of other deities – Brahma, Rudru, up to the Mahakala Itself …

From somewhere in that bag of tricks, the shaft of

the slant-bolt lock rattles in its latch. The door, which had been cold to the touch up until now, begins to warm.

Just as Dawn and Sardar believe they might get into the house with a mystic rebar, Dawn feels an unseen object strike her in the torso. Screaming, she lifts her shirt to find a bloody wound on her stomach. It looks like stigmata – a puncture wound without a puncture.

"Sardar," she rasps.

He says, "Oh my God, look at this. You're in no condition to go in there now. I need to get you to help."

Sardar lifts Dawn and carries her back to the car kicking and screaming.

"What are you doing? My daughter is so close. This may be her last chance. Please!"

"No. I'll come back and handle it on my own."

"You have to wait for me."

"No, it's up to me now. This whole town could come apart if I don't. You, I'm getting to a hospital."

Sardar carries her off and she finally relaxes in his arms.

As she loses consciousness, she remembers the last time she held her stomach in dread, the day she gave birth to Kris and made a promise to Kali …

Chapter 18
Do You Hear the Drums?

Twenty minutes have gone by, and now even Red Herring has lost hope of ever seeing Munzi again. She trails Kris like a hatchling duck in its mother's wake. Kris, not just relaxed but utterly nonchalant, proceeds to the least hideous bathroom they have encountered and jumps in the shower. Red, scared to be alone, follows Kris into the bathroom and stays perched on the toilet seat lid until the gang leader is done.

If she was scared before, she is petrified now as Kris emerges from the shower with blue spots all over her dripping-wet body. Red wonders if the blue is due to some impurity in the water, some parasite that has been breeding in the water main that hasn't been tapped in who-knows-how-long. She' afraid to say a word.

But on closer inspection, the spots are not on Kris's skin, but under it. A thinning veneer of flesh is covering less and less of the cyan pigment.

The blue spots are growing fast enough for Red Herring to bear witness.

Kris, however, is either oblivious to the metamorphosis or uninterested in it.

She says, "Honey, I know you're frightened. But we're gonna get through this. Together."

"Leave me alone!" Red retorts.

"You don't mean that. You're just saying it because you're scared out of your mind." Seeing that Red is unyielding, she offers consolingly, "The blue skin thing is still bothering you, isn't it? I'm a hemophiliac."

"Really?"

"Yes!"

"I'm sorry." It's not that Kris's assertion sounds even the slightest bit convincing. But Red wants to believe.

Gently, Kris says, "Red, did you really lock us in here?"

"No! How would I figure something like that out? I don't even know how to drive. My mom was going to teach me ... She's dead."

Kris' voice is soft, barely audible. "I know that."

Red Herring sobs into her hands. "She took all those pills when I was twelve. She wouldn't have done that if she loved me."

Kris pats Red Herring's shoulder reluctantly, not wanting to step into the role of her mom. She'd rather be the mentor. She says, "Look, whatever you've been through, I've been through worse.

Red Herring looks up, irritated. "You always say that, and you never say why."

Kris's eyes go somewhere else, searching the emptiness inside her. "Whatever happened to me was so bad I blocked it all out. Maybe I was sexually abused..."

"My parents dressed me as a boy!"

"Mine… could be worse."

"But you don't know anything for sure. Your suffering is not real."

Kris stands. "Well, you don't know what it's like not to remember anything."

"Nothing? At all?"

"At least you have bad memories. I have flashes of

what I think may be my past. Terrible."

Just then, the flashes play out for her.

Green water. ... A long trip through a garden ... A woman standing above her with some sort of blunt instrument in her hand, poised to strike ... That house!

"Mine is worse," Red asserts. "Before my mom died, she made me into some smart-alec goody-three-shoes, the freak of the litter. I have to deal with your gang girls taunting me."

"So all I did for you was take advantage of your weakness? Is that what you're saying?"

"No. I mean we all have something to deal with. A dark part of our personality. Something we don't show to the outside world. Waiting to come out."

"You think I asked for this memory lapse? Do you think I like living this blank existence?"

"I wish I could wipe out my pain. I want to run far away, and not just from this house. Do you have a plan to get us out of here?"

"I don't know if there is a way out. It almost feels like we're being punished by some strange force. I feel it, don't you?"

Red doesn't like where the new tone of the conversation has surfaced, from natural to supernatural. "Well, I was just saying..."

"I'm glad you feel it, too. Can you hear the drums, Red? Kris hears Indian music, coming up, getting louder.

"I don't hear anything. You're starting to get to me, Kris." Red Herring tries to back further into the corner. "I want to go to a different room from you, okay?"

Kris bristles at that suggestion until it seems that

another person is emerging from her depths. She growls, "You were the one I was considering keeping alive."

Red tries to back away, but she has nowhere to go.

Whatever is eating Kris recedes for the moment, but it's far from gone. "There is something inside me, Red. Bubbling and trying to tear its way out. Can you hear the screams?"

"Whose screams?"

"The screams of Munzi, Nada, Tamara, and Patti—They're with me. I have a destiny, Red. I may not have a past, but I have a very potent future. Can you hand me my skirt, Red?"

Red passes her the skirt not noticing that it has inexplicably changed to a leopard print. Parts of it are beginning to grow fur like the garment worn by goddess Kali. But the young gang girl wouldn't know about things like that.

Chapter 19
Too Dangerous Even for You

At the rear of house, heat ripples off the building. But it shouldn't. Not in the autumn chill of Massachusetts. Below that, Sardar, hefting a great twisted staff, assembles his dance troupe for a grand scale exorcism. There are literally dozens of young women congregating on the lawn. These are not the kind of girls who entertain at Sardar's sordid club. These are well-bred, respectable young ladies from Cambridge or Newton. With enough money and enough standing in the Indian-American community – both of which Sardar can lay claim to – it is difficult but not impossible to mass an array of dance troupes who know how to expertly perform Bhangra routines.

The dancers wear a time-honored uniform of saffron skirts, gold halters and bejeweled breastplates. Some are stretching out, others are practicing intricate moves that they need to smooth out; a few are simply hanging out, drinking a soda or reading a magazine. None of them are actually paying attention to Sardar, as their agreed-to start time is still more than ten minutes away. If they know what's in store and what's at stake they don't fully believe it will penetrate their bullet proof youth.

Marsha, equipped with an ancient research text, asks, "All these preparations, Sardar… Is there really any way we can stop Kali?"

Sardar assures her blandly, "There is no way to stop

Kali."

"Then what are we doing here, Sardar?"

"An exorcism on this house. Free whichever girls have survived. Maybe save us all. We need a kind of *yantra*, a sound formula."

Sardar begins to draw on the door of the house in chalk in the heart-of-the-house pattern.

"What will it do?"

"Yantras return us to the beginning of time to permit communication with the Divine." Sardar draws as he speaks.

Marsha, anxious to show Sardar her book, says, "Shouldn't we review what we're doing?"

Sardar pushes the book away, and responds with high-pitched irritation. "I don't need to review. You wanted to learn, now pay attention to me. This is the *Raja Yantra* symbol," he says, indicating a design on his ceremonial shield. It is a hexagrammatic representation of a star, a popular design among ancient cultures, all of which have attached mystical meaning to it. "This is what psychic investigators call The Heart of the House."

"The middle?"

"No, the heart, wherever that may be. It's our guideline through the electromagnetic fields. We'll use it to find the source of the power."

Calling out to his team on the great lawn, he says, "I will need six girls in motion at all times."

This gets the reluctant crew to nod and begin to form up. They throw in a few experimental twirls. As Sardar had already explained to Marsha, the configuration represents the six missing girls. "Start now!" he cries.

The exorcism music opens low and begins to rise, the

ancient *tumbi* strings carrying the melody. Marsha believes she is hearing the sounds of the beginning of Indus Valley culture. One of the secrets that Sardar has chosen not to share is that the music is incidental. The real magic stems from the life force of the dancers – not even of the dance. Bhangra is simply the pop music scene that Sardar embraced in his youth while his Western contemporaries were listening to Michael Jackson's *Thriller*.

Staggered by the immensity of their attempt, Marsha pleads, "Sardar, this is a pretty good book." He has spent so long denying her that Marsha has had to study on her own.

"Ignoring her, and pointing at the diagram with his chalk, Sardar instructs, "Listen to me. The intersection of two lines are called *bhedana*, the piercings. The juncture points are *sanhi*, the unions."

"How do you know when you locate Kali?"

"When three lines cross, a sensitive point, *marma*, is formed." He locates it for her and draws the point. "There. But we have not arrived at it yet."

Touching his shoulder with concern, Marsha says, "This is too dangerous, Sardar. Even for you."

Sardar watches the otherworldly ripples torture the house, and replies stoically, "We must rid this place of evil."

Chapter 20
Meet Kris-Kali

Kris drags Red Herring down the hall with her, a rag doll to Kris's growing force. She happens upon another bathroom where she shoves Red into the far corner, then blocks the way back to the door. "Get over there and stay."

Kris looks in the mirror, hauling her shirt and bra off angrily to reveal more extensive changes, and fixes her make-up again. Every time she gazes back in the mirror, more and more spots of blue multiply on her skin – not just in new places, but also in places she has already powdered over.

The drums in her mind grow louder and the beat quickens.

Kris regards herself in disbelief. The transformation has gone too far to ever hide and she is beginning to find that she no longer wants to. More pounding drum runs assault her temples. She puts her head down to endure it as Red stays seated on the edge of the tub. Kris wonders why her follower doesn't hear the deafening beat.

Yet Red Herring notices something because she cries, "What's happening to you?

The drums reach a crescendo, then stop.

Kris looks once more in the mirror to reveal she is now midnight blue from head to toe, and her snakelike necklace has now been replaced by one that has a shrunken skull as a charm. It dangles down to her waist where a full-on leopard skin is now wrapped. Her eyes and eyelids are red with yellow orbs slitted vertically like a cat's. Kris no longer exists. She is Kali, and she takes her place as the most powerful of all goddesses.

Into the silence, Kali roars like a true queen of beasts, and admires the echoes down the hall. She pauses to enjoy the way the walls and floors shake at her fierce war cry.

Red Herring, in a blind-brave panic, ducks around the self-satisfied goddess and sprints out of the room.

BEN PARRIS and WILLIAM FREEDMAN

Chapter 21
How the Witch Broke Out

Interlude: What Has Gone Unsaid

In 2012, a year shy of her parole hearing, a solid psychic connection to her daughter's new activities and the place she was headed for made Dawn arrange for her own "early release." The wait had been worth it. She turned then to her fellow inmate's petrified tongue, which she kept in a small plastic container, and occasionally took out to run against an old piece of leather she used as a strop. With each stroke her power grew.

Sometimes the pointy tongue actually "spoke" to her. It said "kill."

And that day she said, "I will."

Now she gave the dear thing a handle and told it what it needed to do. Stabbing a prison guard with the sharpened tongue, Dawn slipped like an impossibly thin snake through a pipe that took her all the way to the other side of the courtyard and beyond. From there she cast a spell so that the jailers would think she was indeed paroled and that her cellmate did the stabbing.

When night fell, Dawn made her way back to town through a vast field of long, concealing grasses. That's when she heard the music of Sardar's establishment. Emerging in the lot, she saw the sign that identified the place as his. Perfect. She had the guilt card to play against this soft touch of a man. He would do her bidding for sure. Find that daughter she needed and free her from

Kali's grasp. The jail breaker went in with a smile.

Chapter 22
The Dark Butterfly

The time is now, the fish named Sardar is hooked, and the mood is urgent. Dawn is not there in person but no matter. She knows that Gary's heritage just might be strong enough to carry them through. There is important magic yet to be done, and for that, she needs Kris free.

Sardar's Indian dancers writhe to the beat of the loud, exotic music, their dance's origins lost in an antiquity that the Western world cannot comprehend. Sardar chants to the sky, "I invoke the power of Brahmin. You are the dark butterfly, You are the green parrot with red eyes, the thunder cloud, the seasons, the seas. Womb and tomb of the Universe, smite her!" He rounds out his plea with a solid thump of his staff in the grass, which makes Marsha jump. Sardar is good but he hasn't got it yet.

Marsha brandishes her book, angling for her boss's attention. "But Brahmin is the wrong god for this, Sardar. There are a lot of other good ones in here."

"Like what?"

Stabbing her finger at the line art in the book, she says, "What about Subrahmanya? He's the God of War. And he hates women. He'll fight her."

"Nonsense," says Sardar. "Brahmin is the penicillin of gods. It has to do something!"

Chapter 23
Dance of the Damned

Red Herring plunges willy-nilly down the stairs, skids around the turn at the landing, and arrives panting at the door, only to find it sealed as before. She throws herself at this stubborn egress, desperate to get out while a blonde, dark blue Kali clad only in a skull necklace and a swath of leopard skin on her hips, with her yellow and red cat eyes ablaze, chases her.

The front entrance locks three ways, top, bottom and middle, but none of the latches are actually in a locked position. Still, the dumb door does not give, no matter how hard Red pushes or pulls.

The goddess takes her time, savoring the chase of a cornered prey. Besides, there is a ceremony to be had. Unhurried, she dances her way down the stairs using movements that the troupe outside would find familiar, the nightmare flip side of what they are doing. Kali swings a noose to the most hair-raising sounds Red ever heard. If it were not so loud, not so thick with the subtext of undistilled evil, the swoop of her cord would sound like a demon baby's rattle.

But there is more to Kali's slow step than enjoying the terror of the moment. Kali's performance of the Dance of The Damned is an essential ritual before her killing can begin. The theme song of terror is no longer confined to Kali's head. Although Red Herring is too overcome with the flight impulse to wonder where the music is coming from, she hears it blaring her doom as well. Kali is stiff when the composition runs slowly but fluid when the chorus pipes in. At the bottom of the stairs, she casts down the noose and turns to reveal a dagger that she draws in one graceful swipe to the last of the straining notes. She is two feet from her suffering prey.

Over the exorcism music, Sardar gathers himself and intones, "I call Brahmin Immortal, Primal Being. You are the master of her. Break her hold. Break her hold!"

Behind a frustrated Marsha, a line of six remaining dancers poses in genuflection, swinging their long, raven hair in side-to-side in unison with the music's undulations. Unknown to Sardar, Marsha and the massed dancers, their efforts are beginning to have the desired effect.

An explosive sound shakes the yard, the sound of the mystical seal breaking and the door flying open to snap against the other side of the house. Sardar is too deeply entranced to notice it. Kali still occupies Kris's body, but at least the house has found the fortitude to expel the evil deity.

With no time to spare, the door gives way for Red Herring, no thanks to her desperate shoves. Red pounds her way down the winding outside steps. The monster emerges behind her, slightly disoriented to be out in the world, adding her heat ripple to the bright sunlight. Then suddenly focused on nothing but the acquisition of her prey, she is off in a slap-footed run, slamming the pavement like a being of animated stone. Concrete and macadam buckle and crack under the strain.

Kali is no longer playing. The dance is over. Now that her moment of disorientation is over, she breaks into a run after Red, who has taken the opportunity to open up a twenty-yard lead.

Marsha shouts at Sardar across the back lawn, "Something is wrong!"

"Not now, Marsha!" he replies, barely hearing her words over the music he has selected for the dancers.

"I heard a sound. You should stop for a minute."

"I am trying to concentrate," he screams.

More girls join the dance as it becomes more complicated. They pirouette – or the equivalent – holding their arms up in, fingers splayed delicately, in the graceful fashion unique to India's tradition of dance. Yet they find it more difficult than any marathon practice session they've ever faced.

Red shortcuts the road, taking the grass past a dead willow in the midst of a profusion of life. Kali stays close on her, never more than a few paces behind. Kali at that point comes to grips with her mortal form. Kris has never been a fast runner. None of the girls whose souls she has just feasted upon were. But they were, on a whole, physically strong. Patti less so, but no weakling. Kris and Munzi definitely capable of handling themselves in a contest of might. And then there was Nada, whose strength alone matched all the others. Calling upon this gift of strength, Kali uproots a stout pear tree, as if it were weak with age and brittle with the chill. She hurls the entire tree, wildly missing Red Herring. She literally does not yet know her own strength.

But just as Red breathes a sigh of relief that the trunk of the tree missed her skull by at least a foot and a half, she fails to notice a branch that splintered off and tumbled into her path at shin height. Red's foot hooks under the branch and she takes a tumble.

This length of wood gives Kali a wicked idea to increase her accuracy. She then snaps off two hefty branches and whips them in all directions like a vicious pair of *nunchaku*. With each swipe they produce a most satisfying whistle. The open air is – she has to stipulate – good for her. Her face contorts into what Red interprets as a grimace of hatred and bloodlust. But she is merely smiling.

Red rises and takes a few running steps down the road. Kali heaves one of her branches and bowls the young gang girl down. It is time to end this troublesome, last-to-die Red Herring, and to that end Kali runs her down before Red can gather herself again. Kali's legs in stomping mode are quick. Mortal organs on mortal girls do not stand a chance against them. Trapped on the ground, a resourceful animal at bay, this youngest of gang girls twitches away from the sandaled feet again and again, but she cannot last long.

Thundering, god-caliber percussion rumbles through the exorcism music. The dancing demon-ridders shift into a pattern of forming lines, morphing to wide rings, then run together into the middle of the circle to spin and explode outward again into a set of arcane symbols. With each iteration, there are fewer dancers available. They are dying off from the strain one by one. The routine is physically exhausting in itself, but the battle to contain the evil takes a mystic toll that none of them have experienced in their young lives. This burden takes the form of internal bleeding, then external bleeding, and eventually vomiting their guts onto their elaborate saffron costumes. The last thing they hear is Kali's music drowning out Sardar's.

Chapter 24
Pizza Break!

Sardar keeps replacing girls; he requires one more dancer in motion for everyone who succumbs.

A van drives around the road's bend, the vehicle's driver not even noticing the orgy of fatal dance, but Marsha sees him. Unknown to her, it is the pizza boy whom Munzi called way back when they broke into the house. The same one who called back right after the Munz got crushed. *Bup-a-bup, a-buh buh buh bum…* Although she didn't pick up, he eventually came anyway.

The newcomer wears horn-rimmed glasses and a green "I [Heart] the Monster Hero" T-shirt that reminds Marsha of the one that a character named Arbie wore in her guilty-pleasure movie, *Poultrygeist: Night of the Chicken Dead*. Marsha wonders if she should interrupt Sardar again, as he is oblivious to this new development.

The pizza boy unerringly takes the back road to the old reception building for the B & B. When he emerges, he struggles to balance three pie boxes while tilting at the balky sliding van door, and rechecks the address taped to the top of his stack. "Where the fuck am I?"

Cheering himself up as he gets the whole assembly squared, he says, "I am so glad I'm delivering pizza rather than that awful chicken I used to serve. I love the smell of pizza."

It is a few jolly steps to the action around the bend

from the van. He is insensible to anything but finding the customer he had been searching for in the past who-knew-how-many hours since the now-dead Munzi called it in. The pizza boy rounds the bend.

Stupidly, he assumes the woman lying sprawled on the ground is his customer. Maybe she looks the type to order pizza from strange locations. Addressing Red Herring, he says, "Are you the one that ordered the extra salty with—"

The sight of the hellish Kali-Monster invading his view stops him. With a growing awareness of his horrible plight, he says, "This may be the wrong address."

Kali, furious at the interruption, lunges. In a single, graceful motion, she swipes away the pizza boxes into a spinning tumble and sinks her teeth into his throat. The erstaz-Arbie flies ten feet backward, the monster attached to him, until they land out of sight in a clutter of trees. In flight, and for a short while afterward, he wails his drawn out, screaming protest that he had the wrong address as if this appeal could stop the attack.

As Red Herring plays dead, all she can hear is Kali pausing for a bone crunching, slobbering, burping snack.

Not satisfied with the taste of pizza boy, Kali rediscovers her previous toy in the road, stomps out, and plants a foot on her neck.

Chapter 25
Kali Begone

Sardar picks up the pace, his dancers thrashing wildly. Sardar himself is traipsing among them, wielding his great beam of a staff with the twisted top. "Brahmin help us!" he cries. Running out of legitimate things to say, he finally takes Marsha's mousy advice and tries a mundane, "We need you!"

Red Herring struggles, pinioned in the road, both hands pushing at the sandal with all her might.

But Kali is not ready to crush down. Her voice is thunder: "When I finish with your mortal meat, you shall be fed upon by vultures and jackals." This too is part of her ceremony, her standard practice.

As Kali looks for her vulture compatriots in the Heavens, Red scrapes herself sideways and out from under the jeweled sandal. She scrambles madly backwards on the grass, ever closer to the exit gate.

Kali-Monster catches up and kicks Red Herring savagely. Red's strikes in return are completely ineffective. In a matter of moments, Red is literally under Kali's heel again, a blue, gold-sandaled foot with crimson toenails choking the fight out of her. Kali picks her foot up to give Red one last taste of air before stomping down on her windpipe.

Just as Kali re-plants her blue foot on Red Herring's throat, and she is about to crush—

Sardar is down to the last six of his girls, the absolute minimum. They look worn and torn like him. The air is simmering and spitting, the sky warping. He has indeed fulfilled a wealth of psychic checkboxes on the cosmic list. He deserves a victory. Sweating profusely, bellowing over the music with all he has left, he goes for the final statement, from which he cannot retreat, commanding, "Kali begone!"

On those words, out of Sardar's line of view, Kali-Monster shakes prodigiously; maybe she will shake apart. Her foot remains on Red Herring's neck all the while, threatening to snap it even in her death throes.

Red struggles to get out from under with the same trick she tried before. She can't because the foot is even lower than it had been when Kali was taunting her.

Kali roars in chorus with the voices of every beast that can vocalize, as if she has swallowed them all at one time or another. Yet as these voices begin to escape her in excruciating deliverance, she weakens and begins to dissolve in a syrupy mess that spills her monstrous gore onto her victim.

From deep inside her scarred past, Red finds strength beyond that which had ebbed out. Taking advantage of the weakened monster, she twists the leg that pins her. It crunches and crackles causing Kali to express the delirious pain of a wounded elephant, a damaged jackal, and all the rest of her pantheon menagerie. Copious slime flows down onto Red's face as the leg detaches. With a final pop, it flops to the road beside Red's disarrayed hair.

Kali fixes her balance on her remaining leg like a hellish blue flamingo, but then shakes and roars anew in exquisite anguish before she gives herself up to the elements in a great, gusting and rising column of smoke. Between the wispy gaps, parts of her vanish and roaring animal voices drop out of the chorus one by one until all her Earthly bits are gone.

Epilogue
You Weren't a Virgin

Dawn is overseeing the workmen scattered about the grounds of Bonnie's, and she has company. The survivors of the horror in those walls are dressed differently these days: Red Herring has traded in her green gang color for a pink that more suits her reddish hair and pale complexion. Dawn wears a short-sleeved top that is flattering and appropriate to a bright, spring morning – but she wears it well, with respectability, a woman of substance. There is no Mighty Sardar bedecked in ceremonial robes, just Gary, the successful day-trader and nightclub hobbyist who is comfortable in his white, linen jacket and gray, twill slacks. They look to the world like one, big, happy family. In truth, Dawn and Gary's relationship is still being defined, but they have successfully petitioned the courts to allow them joint custody of Red as their foster child.

Red, hugging Dawn tightly like it is the restoration of her suicidal mother, says, "I can't believe you bought this place. It's a little weird though, isn't it?" She doesn't finish the thought that it's weird because her friends died there under the new paint job. The twisted, uprooted life she's led has gotten her used to body surfing her fate.

"It was actually Burl's place to begin with," Dawn lies artfully to Red and Sardar. "He started it. I finally inherited it."

"Yes, I figured that," he says.

"How?"

"Burl Bonnie? Bonnie's B&B? You forget, Burl and I were best friends, and I worked here."

A creepy workman in overalls and hip boots interrupts them. "Hey, I found something in your pool. Something big. You better come take a look. I don't get paid for this shit."

They follow the worker back through a wild area on the grounds. Behind the weeds is a flat green expanse that could be taken for moss and mud, but is nothing so solid. Dawn has a good idea where they are going now though she doesn't say a word. She walks as though absorbed in a dream where she cannot exercise any lucid control.

"I fell in here and tripped over this," he says. The rough-hewn man muscles a waterlogged body-sized bag from the overgrown swamp of a fishpond.

Red Herring and Sardar exchange troubled looks. "Maybe we shouldn't open it," says Red.

The workman, however, is looking to Dawn as the owner, and she simply nods. Nothing at this point can stop her day of reckoning.

The bag has a zipper and has not been fully sealed. Murky water has been pouring out since it hit solid land. After a few tugs and a peel back, there is more clearly a human shape obscured by a choke of weeds. The workman scoops away handfuls of soupy plants and dirt to reveal human-form Kris gone pale and gray but for a blue network of veins through translucent skin. She had been missing a quarter century and should have withered to nothing, but curiously she doesn't look that bad to Dawn if she could ignore the swamp plants that have grown into her daughter's flesh. Her open eyes, which should have been the first to go, are white as milk.

Dawn crouches over the body in a curious state of detachment. "It's my girl. Kris. She's been dead a long time."

Red finally finds her voice and screams, not only because it's Dawn's Kris but because it's her Kris too, complete with her gang shirt and snake necklace.

Dawn says, "This one didn't make much of a goddess, did she?" Stroking Kris's medusa tangle of hair gently, she raises her voice to shrill proportions, "My daughter... she wasn't a virgin." She directs her sudden anger directly to the corpse. "That's what went wrong," she shouts. "You weren't a virgin!"

Dawn reaches into the body bag, and removes the eye club that had kept Kris in a preserved state. One hand clings to the stick before it falls away. Free of the club and its spell, Kris's eyes return to normal in a few blinks, whereupon she sputters and begins to wake. "Mom?"

Red Herring and Sardar look at each other in astonished joy. Even though Dawn is disturbed, and Kris is a world-class mess, it looks like this encounter will turn into a happy ending.

The startled Dawn recovers fast, raising her eye club high above her head.

Kris is even more confused now, her voice high and plaintive.

"Mom?"

Dawn was in the woods, getting beaten by Burl.

In between strikes at her, Burl said, "I told you ... to lay off ... the supernatural ... Dawn."

Dawn yelled, "Don't! No one has to know!" When he did not relent, she said, "I'll get you for this."

She kicked him and he flew through the air to land on his back, licking his bloody lips. In terror he stared at a transformed beast that approached him — Kali's loaner body to Dawn from one of her many manifestations — and as the inhuman roar issued from its lips he added his own terrified song.

Dawn foresees the discovery of Burl's body next, as she has placed him in the swampy pond right next to her discarded daughter. *Act quickly,* says an echo of Kali. Dawn raises the eye club high, becoming very decisive now. On the downswing, Dawn stabs her daughter in the chest as if she were staking a vampire. *Ka-chunk.* It's the exact same sound that its identical companion pole made when it went through Tamara. Red is soaked in a wild spray of whatever swamp blood was running through Kris' veins. She can't stop shrieking now.

Sardar, who was resplendent in white, makes an even better splatter canvas, yet he barely notices. He restrains Dawn when he sees what she's done, but one blow to the heart was enough. He is too late. "What did you do?" he cries. "What could you possibly hope to gain?"

Dawn explains, "I invoked the Goddess of time and change. I wanted eternal energy, perpetual life." Addressing her daughter again, she pleads, "Why do you keep surfacing? Why can't you stay dead?"

"You were lying the whole time," says Sardar. "You were the worshipper. You did the sacrifice. Burl didn't kill anyone, did he?" Shaking her insensate form, he demands, "Did he?"

"Don't blame me. She needed to be a virgin. This is

all your fault."

The pool man says, "There's another bag here too." Without asking permission, he hauls the bag further out for their inspection, and does another unzip.

Red Herring covers her mouth. "Oh no, no."

Sardar digs into the bag, his face darkening with grim determination as he zeroes in to confirm, "It's Burl."

Idea for the Sequel:
No Rest Home for the Wicked

Seventy-five-year-old Gary is many years past his days as The Mighty Sardar. Some people at his age are much better off than they had been in earlier life. Not Gary. Crumpled in his backless hospital gown, white bearded, confined to a wheelchair, he is a shadow of his former self. All he looks forward to nowadays are chocolate pudding, some TV, and rummaging through the memories of his experiences with the supernatural, a hard life.

Most important is the comforting thought that those days of meatball hocus pocus are behind him. Not too much has changed in the town of Salem since he caught their last real witch, Dawn. They've gone back to their New-Age and wiccan boutiques and their playful broomstick signage that wows the tourists. That fact warms Gary. She is gone. He's done a good job. Did the right thing. He is a hero.

No one in Salem could blame him for the tragedy of twenty-five years ago.

His chair comes to a halt. He hadn't even realized that someone was wheeling him through the hall.

"You got a light?" A man named Damon Heckler, in another wheelchair, asks.

"You?" Gary says, looking up. This is the perpetually old man he'd seen in his club night after night, tormenting him since the beginning of his career on stage. Still here, and now they are the same age.

Damon lights up a vapor cigarette with the tip of his

finger and blows the smoke into a pitchfork shape.

"You can't smoke in here," Gary sputters. "It's a freakin' hospital."

Damon laughs. "You know I'm not really here, Sardar. I'm a product of your meds."

"What were you before that?" Gary blinks. Damon cackles and vanishes.

The wheelchair's wheels spin, jerking Gary toward another corridor, a dark one.

"Fuck."

Hoping the meds will clear through, Gary puts his head down again, and in his stomach, a terrible acid forms. He sighs.

"Dementia," he says to himself, knowingly. "And probably diarrhea."

The blonde nurse shakes her head at his foolishness and continues to push Gary along. It is gang girl Kris, twenty-years-old, her face turned a familiar shade of blue. "Here," she says, "let me make you more comfortable." And she yanks the pillow out from under his light frame, crams it over his face and puts him out of his misery.

Boom go the paddles, delivering their electric shock. Sardar's back arches like London Bridge. London Bridge falling down.

The attendant is some kind of bizarre Las Vegas super nun, trimmed in red and glitter-gold with a flipped up lapel and a white scarf. "You're not going anywhere, you old fucker." She fixes her collar, spits on each paddle, rubs them together, and digs in again. Boom!

Sardar wakes, sits up high on the bed and says, "Hey, get off me. Stop that. What is this? St. Elvis Fire? Dammit, I was all ready to die."

"So sad, too bad."

"Wait a minute," he points accusingly, "I know you. I've seen a picture of you. You're one of those crude-talking gang girls that stirred up all the trouble. You're The Munzi."

"I'm known as Saint *Nun*zi now. I always said it could happen. Now I'm an envoy attached to the spirit world. And I'm still cool." She tugs at her lapel collar with pride. "Anyway," she says, taking out a cell phone, "I got an emergency text about you."

"You have a cell phone?"

"Duh! I get H-Mobile up there! It's great."

"This is so crazy, I just wet myself. You can't really be here."

She shrugs. "Huh, well it could be the meds I suppose."

"What do you want with me?"

"Oh yeah. The Powers that Be are putting you back in service. Kali is roaming the Earth. She actually killed you a few minutes ago. You're going to have to fight her again."

"I'm in no shape to do that."

"One more jolt of this saint juice, and you'll feel like a new man." She winks as she moves in with the paddles again. "Try not to cry like a bitch."

ABOUT THE AUTHORS:

Ben Parris is a contributor/ editor of anthologies *Drastic Measures* and *Wash the Spider Out*. Parris is the author of two screenplays including *Dmitriev*, a TBS made-for-television movie, and the movie version of *Supernaturalz: Weird Creepy & Random* as well as several other novels. As an article writer, he has interviewed and written about science fiction icons such as actor Michael York and *Star Trek* writer George Clayton Johnson for a multi-part series in *Screem Magazine*.

William Freedman is a New York-based satirist who uses science fiction and fantasy tropes. In that vein, he is author of *Mighty Mighty* and *Land That I Love*. Most recently, he served as editor for the *Age of Certainty: What if God Existed?* anthology. His non-fiction, including coverage of the Bram Stoker Awards weekend for Long Island's *Newsday*, goes back more than 20 years.

CAST OF THE MOVIE

Lucy Spain..................Kris, Kali, and Swamp Kris
Debbie D...Dawn
Alexia Anastasio..........….................Red Herring
Tationna Bosier.................................Tamara
Amanda Marcheschi............…..................Munzi
Mia Bené..Nada
Courtney Klotz.....................................Patti
Paulson Ambookan.................….....The Mighty Sardar
Pamela Zwaskis...................................Marsha
Joel M. Reed...........................Damon Heckler
Joe Zaso..Burl
Jason Yachanin...............................Pizza Guy
Frances Pabón...................................Singer
Cynthia Shaw.......................................Witch
Alisa Lova..Maris
Shane McGowan..............................Pool Man
Jonathan Hart.........…................... Young Gary
Marisol Cahill....................…....…....Snake Girl/ Anita
Caity Guinn.............................Princess Sultana
Mira Gutoff........................…..........Waitress
Neil Iorio........................…......Bar Patron
William Freedman............................Bar Patron

www.ingramcontent.com/pod-product-compliance
Lightning Source LLC
Chambersburg PA
CBHW061730020426

42331CB00006B/1186